THEN AND THERE SERIES
GENERAL EDITOR
MARJORIE REEVES

G000126275

Village Life in the Eighteenth Century

HERBERT GREEN

Illustrated from contemporary sources

LONGMAN

LONGMAN GROUP LIMITED
London
*Associated companies branches and representatives
throughout the world*

First published 1976
Second impression 1978
ISBN 0 582 22122 6

*Printed in Hong Kong by
The Hong Kong Printing Press (1977) Ltd*

For Elizabeth

Contents

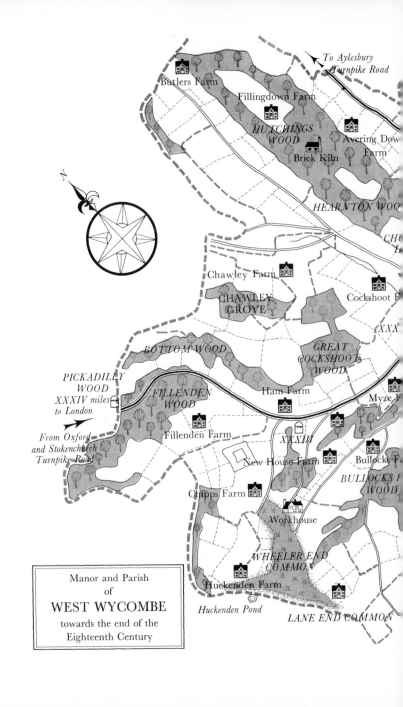

To Aylesbury
Turnpike Road

Butlers Farm

Fillingdown Farm

*HUTCHINGS
WOOD*

Avering Dow
Farm

Brick Kiln

HEARNTON WOO

CH

Chawley Farm

*CHAWLEY
GROVE*

Cockshoot E

XXX

BOTTOM WOOD

*GREAT
COCKSHOOT
WOOD*

*PICKADILLY
WOOD*
XXXIV *miles*
to London

*FILLENDEN
WOOD*

Ham Farm

Myze E

From Oxford
and Stokenchurch
Turnpike Road

Fillenden Farm

XXXIII

New House Farm

Bullocks F.

*BULLOCKS
WOOD*

Chipps Farm

Workhouse

*WHEELER END
COMMON*

Huckenden Farm

Manor and Parish
of
WEST WYCOMBE
towards the end of the
Eighteenth Century

Huckenden Pond

LANE END COMMON

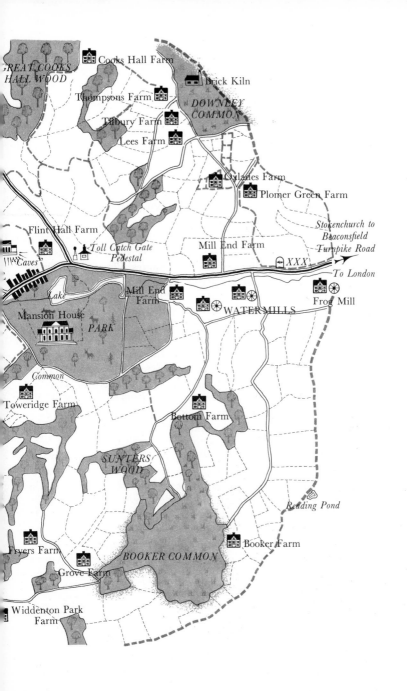

GREAT COOKS
HALL WOOD

Cooks Hall Farm

Brick Kiln

DOWNLEY
COMMON

Thompsons Farm

Tilbury Farm

Lees Farm

Oxlades Farm

Plomer Green Farm

Flint Hall Farm

Stokenchurch to
Beaconsfield
Turnpike Road

Toll Catch Gate
Pedestal

Mill End Farm

Caves

XXX

To London

Lake

Mill End
Farm

WATER MILLS

Frog Mill

Mansion House

PARK

Common

Toweridge Farm

Bottom Farm

SUNTERS
WOOD

Reading Pond

Fryers Farm

Booker Farm

Grove Farm

BOOKER COMMON

Widdenton Park
Farm

To the Reader

In the Chiltern Hills of Buckinghamshire, some thirty miles north-west of London, lies the village of West Wycombe, surrounded by *parish* and *manor*, over 6,000 acres of meadow, pasture, cornfields, woods and hills. A small stream known in the eighteenth century as the mill-brook and in modern times as the River Wye, begins its short journey of less than ten miles to the River Thames. Through the parish too runs the A40 road, for centuries one of the main routes from London, stream and road at no point far apart. Most of the houses in the village of West Wycombe are in the main street lining the two sides of the A40 where it runs at the foot of Church Hill, with the church of St Lawrence, rebuilt in the eighteenth century, on its summit. There is no other church quite like it. On the other side of the valley to the south of the main street lies West Wycombe Park. On rising ground in the park, stands West Wycombe House. Here Sir Francis Dashwood, *premier baronet of Great Britain*, lives with his family, and here Dashwoods have lived for three hundred years.

Deeds, letters, account books and other papers of many kinds, tell the story of Sir Francis Dashwood, lord of the manor of West Wycombe from 1724 to 1781, and other lords of the manor before and after him. The parish records tell the story of other people on the manor; the middling sort who paid *poor rate* and *church rate* and who might be called upon to be churchwarden, overseer of the poor, surveyor of the highways, or *petty constable*; the labouring poor, who fared hard and often suffered want.

Remember in those days the value of money was very different: it is not possible to say how much £1 then would represent now. Many things we buy now, eighteenth-century people could not buy at all: they did not exist. Here are specimen prices in Berkshire, you can see how they rose in the space of fifty years:

	About 1750	1797
Bread, half-peck loaf	8*d*	1*s*
Beef and mutton per lb	3*d*	5*d*
Cheese per lb	3*d*	5*d*
Butter per lb	5*d*	10*d*
Sugar per lb	3*d*	8*d*
A foulweather coat	12*s* 0*d*	22*s* 0*d*

A labourer generally earned 1*s* per hour, and a craftsman earned 1*s* 6*d*. The rent for a poor cottage was about 3*s* a year and for a better cottage or house was about £3. A good way to compare prices at various times is to work out how long people had to work to buy what they needed.

Words printed in *italics* in the text are explained in the Glossary, on page 91.

I An Eighteenth-century Visitor to West Wycombe

THE JOURNEY

On Wednesday, 4 October 1752, Thomas Phillibrown and friends left London at quarter-past-seven in the morning bound for High Wycombe. Soon after six o'clock in the evening they were at the King's Head at Beaconsfield, and by a little after ten, having eaten a supper of two roast chickens, were in bed. Next day they arrived at the Swan at High Wycombe, by twelve noon. Luckily for us, Thomas Phillibrown kept a diary, which we can still read. Between 1750 and 1758 he made five journeys to High Wycombe, for business and pleasure. His business was to collect money from customers he had supplied with wine: his pleasure, to walk in the countryside around.

Thomas Phillibrown travelled by horse transport of one kind or another: on horseback or, when ladies were in the party, in a four-wheeled carriage with a pair of horses, and on his last visit, in a coach with four horses. The eighteenth century was the century of the horse. In 1798 there were more horses (163 with 92 wagons and carts) in West Wycombe than labourers (141). Besides these horses, there would be horses at inns to be hired by travellers, and at West Wycombe House horses for riding and hunting. As the road from London to Oxford and beyond formed the main street of the village, scores if not hundreds of horses must have passed through daily, and, even before the eighteenth century, on a special occasion as many as fourteen coaches and thirty horses had

Opposite: *The church of St. Lawrence in West Wycombe. Notice the golden ball on the top of the tower, you can still see it today*

been seen at one time going down a hill to the west of the village.

THE CHURCH WITH THE GOLDEN BALL

During Thomas Phillibrown's second visit to High Wycombe, he was persuaded to ride to West Wycombe to see Sir Francis Dashwood's estate, 'exceedingly fine and pleasantly situated'. From the road in West Wycombe village, Phillibrown had a charming view of 'a large piece of water' which Sir Francis had had made by damming the little river. On the lake were several small boats. But it was the church on the hill high above village and park, which fascinated the London wine merchant:

With some difficulty and a little fear, we at last arrived

at the Church which is situated on a very high Chalk hill, the Tower of which Church Sir Francis has (at his own expense) for the sake of a prospect to his House and Gardens, raised to twice the height it was before and on the top of the said tower is building a spire of timber, on the top of which is built of wood a very large hollow globe, the diameter of which is 8 feet and the outside of it is to be covered with gilt. We just went within the Church and up as high as the bell loft but had not the courage to ascend higher.

Six years later, when Thomas Phillibrown visited West Wycombe again, Sir Francis Dashwood had finished the golden ball on the top of the church tower.

Mr Richardson went up ye ladder and out on ye leads of ye steeple, to view ye going up into ye great gilded ball. I afterwards took courage and went quite round the leads tho with great fear and trembling for the great height makes it quite shocking. We neither of us had the courage to enter the ball which is considerably higher from the leads of the steeple: ye going up is on ye outside of a wooden spire with clamps of wood nailed like a ships side and ye ropes to take hold of it and a part of ye ball lifts up into which you can enter. We heard after that our coachman went into it. It is very large and said to hold 20 persons; there is a table in ye middle, seats around it and windows at ye top. Sir Francis with 12 or 13 of his friends has been up in ye ball at one time and drank *punch* there.

Why did Sir Francis Dashwood place a golden ball on top of the church?

In 1676 an Italian artist had built a golden ball on the customs house in Venice. Paintings of Venice by Vanvitelli and Canaletto show this ball. It was probably the memory of the gilded copper ball, seen by Sir Francis while in Italy, that made him build the golden ball on West Wycombe church.

The golden ball on the Customs House in Venice

THE FINE HOUSE AND PARK OF THE LORD OF THE MANOR

From the church Thomas Phillibrown and his friend had an excellent view of Sir Francis Dashwood's house and gardens and of the surrounding fields and hills topped with beech woods, their leaves turning from summer's green to autumn's yellow, brown and burning gold or red in the rays of the sinking sun. He says in his diary:

> We saw many pheasants in a place kept on purpose for their breeding. On ye Grand Canal are great numbers of wild ducks and in it great quantities of fish; and in a bason

A photograph of West Wycombe House, part of the park and the village taken from the air. The scene must have been very much the same in the eighteenth century

of water facing ye greenhouse are great numbers of gold and silver fish from India. In ye Grand Canal are various vessels, one of which is a *Snow*, Burthen about 60 Tun; it is compleatly rigg'd and carries several brass carriage guns which were taken out of a French *Privateer* and a sailor constantly is kept who lives aboard this snow to keep it in proper order; we all went on board it and there is a neat pretty cabin, *forecastle* or cork room and both under decks and outside is neatly painted and everything in quite pretty order and well worth seeing. There are also about three other vessels of various forms, a barge and boats, which little fleet afford an agreeable prospect. There are also swans on ye canal to add to ye beauty. We were told by ye sailor at one time a battery of guns in form of a fort was erected on ye side of ye canal in order to make a sham fight between it and ye little fleet but in ye engagement a Capt. who commanded ye Snow comeing too near ye battery, received damage from ye *wadding* of a gun which occasion'd him to spit blood and so put an end to ye battle.

We have a map, made for Sir Francis Dashwood by his 'most dutiful servant' Morise Lewis Jolivet in 1752. This map, four engravings of the house and park in 1757, and a painting of 1773 give a full picture of the lake, bridges, wooded islands, fort, temple of *Venus*, temple of *Daphne*, bowling green, *cascade*, greenhouses, ornaments, statues, and of course—on rising ground—the house itself. Shown only on the 1752 map on an island in the lake is a *menagerie*. Many of the eighteenth-century landed *gentry* felt that they must have a menagerie to keep up with the others. At High Wycombe, about two and a half miles away, the Earl of Shelburne near his house, now called Wycombe Abbey, had a lion in a den (and paid one shilling for a mop to clean the lion), a beaver and an *orang-outang*, killed in one night by a severe frost. Still in Buckinghamshire, the zeal with which the Duchess of Portland collected wild animals made people say that she was expecting another Great Flood and that like Noah, was collecting every living thing of all flesh after its own kind!

In the picture of West Wycombe Park in 1773 on page 14 you can see, between the lady and children and the deer, a ha-ha, a ditch with one side vertical and bricked, and the other sloping and grassed. When Sir Francis Dashwood created his park, like other landed gentry of his day, he wanted to have an excellent view from his house. At the same time he had to find a way to keep sheep, cattle and deer from straying on to the lawns and coming too near the house. Walls, hedges or fences would have spoilt the view. The ha-ha kept the animals away from the house but could not be seen until you were close up. Why this curious name? It is said that country folk, not the landed gentry, first used the name. Seeing

West Wycombe House, 1773

deer kept away without a wall, hedge or fence to be seen,
'Ha-ha' they said as they came to the sunken wall and ditch
and saw the reason for the mystery.

A map of the manor of West Wycombe drawn about
1708 shows the manor house near the village and the road
from London to Oxford, but no park surrounding it. Instead,
it only shows two lawns and three fields, each called Ironfield,
whatever that may mean. Now Sir Francis wanted a park
round his house, which would give him a fine view. So straight
across the valley of the mill-brook, and within sight of the
house, he built a dam, which held up the waters of the stream

The lake in the park of the manor house in 1757.
Can you see the church on the hill?

until they formed a lake. This was the lake which Thomas Phillibrown called the Grand Canal, a name which probably Sir Francis himself gave it after the Grand Canal in Venice where he had stayed. For years after Phillibrown's visit, Sir Francis continued to improve his grounds and park.

He planted many English trees like beech and oak; trees not native to England he brought direct from Italy along with statues and urns. Almost to his death he continued to build temples in the grounds. When later in his life, as Baron le Despencer, he spent much of his time at West Wycombe, he would look on a scene of great beauty: from the north side of the house, groups of majestic trees, by the lake and climbing church hill across the valley; above the trees the gleaming golden ball perched on the top of the church tower, and to the right of the church, a six-sided building with massive walls of flint, open to the sky, not built when Phillibrown was at West Wycombe—a mausoleum, the word meaning a magnificent tomb: within the mausoleum, are inscriptions (one to Sir Francis himself), an urn in memory of his wife, and monuments for two of his father's four wives. In the six walls are recesses for more urns. On an island in the lake, visible from the north side of the house stood the Temple of Music. Scattered about were *alcoves* and other small buildings intended as garden ornaments and in line with the ha-ha, the Temple of the Winds, a copy of a Greek temple in Athens.

When Sir Francis Dashwood's father died in 1724 he left a plain brick house. Sir Francis did not marry until 1745 when he was thirty-seven years of age. About this time, probably to please his wife, he began to rebuild the house, stage by stage, taking something like twenty-five years. In front of the south side he built columns in two storeys, copied from a building near Venice in Italy built by an Italian, Antonio Palladio, who lived from 1518 to 1580, and who greatly admired the ancient buildings of Rome. On all four sides of the house, Sir Francis erected slender columns and above doors low pitched gables called pediments, triangles with straight sides, all copied from buildings in Greece, Italy and Asia. When Sir Francis had stayed in these countries he had seen temples and palaces built by the Greeks and Romans or by Antonio Palladio.

At each end of the house, Sir Francis had a portico built, a large projecting porch supported by columns. The east portico is a copy of one by Palladio, near Venice, and the west portico a copy of the temple of Bacchus, the Greek god of wine, at Teos in Asia Minor. Nicholas Revett, who built them, and Robert Adam, who planned the stables and kitchen wing, had both been to Greece and Asia Minor to make drawings of ancient buildings. Robert Adams, noted for the elegance of his work, perhaps the most famous architect of the eighteenth century, designed the whole of several important houses, and 16 in London, Edinburgh and many counties in England and

The west portico of the house, which is a very fine copy of ancient Greek architecture

Part of a fresco in West Wycombe House. It shows the wedding of Ariadne and Bacchus

17

Scotland improved houses and public buildings by additions or designs for interiors.

Sir Francis Dashwood brought two painters from Italy, Guiseppe and Giovanni Borgnis, father and son, to paint scenes on walls and ceilings: these pictures were painted before the plaster was dry and are called frescoes. William Hannan, a Scot, painted some of the frescoes in the house. These frescoes were pictures from stories of Greek and Roman gods.

Sir Francis was interested in the gods of the Greeks and Romans as well as their architecture. When the west portico was finished he opened the park to the public for three days and arranged an elaborate *dedication* of the portico, a pagan not a Christian dedication. There was a procession of people dressed as priests and priestesses of *Bacchus* (drunken revellers), Pan (the Greek country god), fauns (country gods with horns and tails), satyrs (woodland gods, half-human, with horses' ears and tails), and Silenus (a rollicking, drunken, bloated old man). After songs of praise to Bacchus, the strangely dressed, roystering folk moved off and wound their way through trees and groves to the head of the lake: here they sang songs of thanksgiving and poured more drink offerings to Bacchus.

In building the house and making the park, Sir Francis Dashwood was following the fashion among eighteenth-century landed gentry of creating beautiful houses and parks and doing it very well. They planted thousands of trees: most were native trees like beeches and oaks with their regular outlines: some were conifers, their rough bark and ragged crowns making a contrast; many were ornamental trees from abroad. Like Sir Francis, these landowners decorated their parks with artificial lakes and watercourses (often called canals), cascades, *grottoes* and *follies*—sham ruins of churches and castles, copies of ancient temples in Italy, Greece and Asia Minor and statues of gods and goddesses.

In 1751 Sir Francis began to rent Medmenham Abbey on the north bank of the Thames, about halfway between the river-ports of Henley and Great Marlow and some seven miles from his house at West Wycombe. The abbey had been a small monastery in the Middle Ages. He repaired part of it, adding a ruined tower and cloister, surrounding them with beautiful gardens, keeping a handsome pleasure boat and building boathouses in the gardens and on the aytes as the islands in the river were called. In 1732 Sir Francis had been one of the founders of the Dilettanti Society for noblemen and gentlemen interested in antique art and classical buildings: the society still exists. Ten years later he had his portrait painted for the society, as a friar. Soon afterwards he started a mock order of monks which met at Medmenham Abbey. A cellar book tells us that he and his friends gave themselves such names as 'Brother John of Henley and Brother John of Aylesury, Thomas de Greys Abbott, Francis of Wycombe'. Magazines, newspapers and a novel of the time printed gossip and hints about happenings at Medmenham, of wild rites, mock-religious services, *black magic* and even of a baboon, dressed as a devil, set free during one of the sham services. For clubs of reckless young men and clubs which made fun of religion, the eighteenth-century name was hell-fire clubs. As time went by the meetings at Medmenham came to be given that name.

At West Wycombe Sir Francis Dashwood himself may have designed, at least in outline, his gardens and park: it seems that for ten or twelve years he employed Thomas Cook, a pupil of the most famous eighteenth-century landscape gardener, Lancelot Brown, who lived from 1715 to 1785 and was nicknamed 'Capability Brown' because when asked for his opinion about a park, he would usually reply that it had 'capabilities'. He designed no less than 140 parks and gardens for dukes and gentlemen in many parts of the country. Examples of his work are the lake at Blenheim Palace, the landscaped park at Luton Hoo in Bedfordshire and the grounds of Glamis Castle in Scotland.

Landed gentry looked for parks not very far from London and from 1760 to 1820 the number of parks in the Chiltern Hills doubled. Some of the nobility had more than one house and park. Lord Lansdowne owned Bowood in Wiltshire and what is now called Wycombe Abbey, some twenty-nine miles 19

The beautiful hall and mahogany staircase in Sir Francis Dashwood's house

from London. The Duke of Portland owned Bulstrode in Buckinghamshire, and Welbeck in the area of Nottinghamshire known as the Dukeries: besides the great houses and parks of the nobility there were many smaller houses and parks of the lesser gentry throughout the country.

2 *The Lord of the Manor*

*Sir Francis Dashwood
(from a portrait
painted in 1761)*

AS A YOUNG MAN—THE GRAND TOUR

Sir Francis Dashwood, the second baronet, lived through most of the eighteenth century. He was born in 1708 and died in 1781. His father, made baronet in 1708, was a merchant trading with Turkey, as was his father before him; both father and grandfather were aldermen of London. Two members of the Dashwood family, which had come up from Somerset, bought the manor of West Wycombe, a convenient day's ride from London, at the turn of the century. In 1726, two years after his father had died, the young Sir Francis Dashwood, who had been to school at Eton, set out on the Grand Tour of Europe, visiting France and returning through Germany. It was the custom for young men whose parents were rich to go on the Grand Tour. (You can read more about this in another Then and There book, 'The Eighteenth-Century Grand Tour'.)

From 1729 to 1731 Francis Dashwood stayed in the Italian cities of Florence and Rome and about two years later, on 10 May 1733, left the Nore in 'the Lowestoft Man of War of twenty guns', becoming probably the first young man to add Russia to the Grand Tour. When he came to rebuild his house at West Wycombe and to make his park, the ideas he had gained as he travelled and saw, read and listened, were given shape.

IN PARLIAMENT

At the age of thirty-three Sir Francis Dashwood became one of the two Members of Parliament for New Romney on the Kent coast. The men allowed to vote numbered only twenty-eight. Sir Francis Dashwood became a candidate for Parliament at New Romney because the Dashwood family had friends there. Dashwood's father had been Member of Parliament for Winchelsea, not far from New Romney. Dashwood's wife's brother had been a New Romney member before him. Elected with Sir Francis was his friend Henry Furnese who had estates and was well known in the town. After Henry Furnese had died, and Dashwood had been member for twenty years, he thought he might not be elected again so he became a candidate for Weymouth and Melcombe Regis on the Dorset coast. After about two years as a member for Weymouth and Melcombe Regis, Sir Francis Dashwood became Baron le Despencer and being now a lord and a member of the House of Lords, he could no longer sit in the House of Commons.

While Sir Francis was still one of the 558 members of the House of Commons, some 350 of the other MPs were landed gentry like him, *squires* to the villagers where they lived. Having a majority they could pass laws to benefit themselves. They did not always do so, and when the country needed money they taxed themselves heavily. They did pass *game* laws which said that only the holders of a considerable area of land could shoot deer, pheasants, partridges, hares and rabbits. The landed gentry appointed gamekeepers to stop men who by shooting or trapping, broke the law. Parliament passed fresh

A poacher caught taking a rabbit from a trap

laws making the punishment for *poachers* more and more severe. Towards the end of the eighteenth century the struggle between gamekeepers and poachers, sometimes in gangs and often with hungry families to feed, became bitter and led to battles. West Wycombe had its gamekeepers and its deer, pheasants, hares, doves, and fish in its streams.

For a short time in 1762–63 Sir Francis Dashwood while still in the House of Commons, was Chancellor of the Exchequer, an office not as important as it is today but important enough. After he had moved to the House of Lords the Prime

23

Minister, William Pitt, Earl of Chatham, made Sir Francis Joint Postmaster-General. He remained in this office until his death fifteen years later receiving a salary of £2,000 a year, with a house in London. He took a keen interest in the many changes which took place in the Post Office, but his duties were light. The Secretary of the Post Office did most of the work and helped to arrange promotion for seven of Dashwood's relations.

Sir Francis encouraged the idea of using postcarts 'to defend the Mails from Rogues and the Weather'. For many years postboys, who might be of any age in spite of their name, carried the mail from one *posthouse* to the next but highwaymen and *footpads* could easily rob the letter bags of the postboys, who were slow, unarmed and often riding old horses. Sir Francis thought that a two-wheeled postcart with a horse trotting between the shafts would be a better way to carry mails. Among the papers of Sir Francis now in the Bodleian Library at Oxford is an estimate for making a postcart and the Secretary of the Post Office sent a postcart to West Wycom-

Post-Boy.

The POST-BOY is a most welcome lad to many a tradesman, when he brings good orders, with a bank-note, or bill to be regularly paid: also to every parent, child, or friend, who wishes to hear of the welfare of parties that live at a distance.

be for Sir Francis to see. A few years after his death in 1781 mail coaches began to carry long-distance mail and it was not long before the London to Shrewsbury and Holyhead mail coach broke the silence of the night as it passed through the village.

A contemporary drawing of a post boy.

AT HOME

The present Sir Francis Dashwood still has an eighteenth-century rent book 4½ inches thick, 13½ inches wide, and 18½ inches long. In this book, a receiver entered rents which Sir Francis Dashwood of that time received and expenses he paid from the rents. Much of the income came from rents paid by tenants on the manor of West Wycombe. Sir Francis allowed the receiver sixpence from every £1 he collected in rent, and over twenty years employed in succession five receivers. William Winter Lawrance was one of these. He lived with his wife in a cottage in the Towne, as the village was called. He became receiver in about 1767 and continued for about ten years. He was also parish clerk. You will read about his work as parish clerk in Chapter 3. A man who could write clearly, spell correctly and add up accounts was very useful in an eighteenth-century village.

The accounts for the year which ended on Lady Day, 25 March 1771, show that the rents due from the twenty or more farms came to £1,562 4s. Not all of the rents due were paid, the collector receiving only £1,320 8s 8¾d. The highest rent was for Flint Hall Farm for which Anne Hurls had to pay £198 12s yearly. (you will read about her later on.) For Chawley Farm Aaron Wooster paid £132 4s and for Fish Mill and a meadow, John Fryer paid £68. Cottages which included inns, alehouse, *malthouses*, a wheelwright's shop and a bakehouse, would bring in £227 16s 6d each year if all rents were paid. For cottages on the commons or waste land the lord of the manor asked for rents varying from one penny to one pound a year, but some of the cottagers did not pay these small sums.

In the Middle Ages the lord of the manor had the right to take the best beast of a tenant who died. On West Wycombe manor in the eighteenth century when a tenant died and another took over his land, the lord of the manor received a sum of money instead of a beast. If land passed from one living tenant to another, the new tenant paid a fine to the lord of the manor. In the West Wycombe rent book fines totalled £2 3s 4d in 1770–71.

In the early Middle Ages too, a person holding land usually did not pay money for the land which he held but worked for the lord of the manor on his land for a few days each week, and gave extra help when there was urgent work like harvesting to do. But as years and centuries went by the lord of the manor preferred to receive money rather than services and the tenants to pay rather than do the work demanded of them. Money paid instead of work was called quit rent. From quit rents in 1770–71 Lord le Despencer received £14 3s 2½d but his tenants still owed him £28 17s 1½d from previous years. Some of them, it would seem, objected to paying quit rents. But all who owed service to Lord le Despencer were summoned to attend a manorial court and pay their quit rents.

A Court Leet was a court held in some manors to deal with petty offences. A Court Baron was an assembly of the tenants of a manor under the lord of the manor or his *steward*. Tenants
26 expected the lord of the manor to give them a special dinner

A notice of Court Leet and Court Baron

each year. When Lord le Despencer did this in October 1770 at the same George Inn, forty-two tenants met to enjoy the annual Court Dinner, for which the lord paid one shilling per head.

The lord of the manor was as keen to prevent the catching of fish without his permission as he was to prevent the poaching of game:

> In 1778 April 22nd. Be it remembered that I John Goodwin of Frog Mill (Paper Maker) in the Parish of West Wycombe in the County of Bucks, Having Contrary to Right and Authority fished the Mill pond of the said Mill, The Right Honourable Lord le Despencer (Lord of the Manor) being informed of the same had ordered a prossicution [prosecu-

tion] to be commenced against me for so doing. But on my waiting on his Lordship He through his wonted goodness had forgiven me the aforesaid offince By an Acknowledgement of one shilling.

JOHN GOODWIN

From the income of the manor the receiver had to pay expenses both small and large. A well bucket cost 4*d*, a 'Well Lidd at Ann Mondays' 1*s* 0*d*, her windows 1*s* 6*d*. Beer and cheese for tenants on rent day £1 1*s* 0*d*, Poors Bread £5 and— as man cannot live by bread alone—£5 for five sermons. The greatest expenditure was on the repair of farms. In one year nine farms had to be repaired, costing £254 in all. There was no income tax in the eighteenth century but Lord le Despencer had to pay land tax—even on empty cottages— and window tax, especially on the windows in the mansion house. In every parish occupiers of land had to pay poor rate for the relief of the poor, and church rate for the upkeep of the parish church and other village and parish expenses, according to the value of the land they occupied. As the lord of the manor occupied more land than anyone else, he paid more poor rate and more church rate.

Farm workers' cottages

In the annual balance of income and expenditure in the rent book occur the words 'Advanced to My Lord at several times'. The amount the receiver gave Sir Francis varied: £1,246 one year, £1,715 another, and as much as £2,536 another. In some years the money paid out was greater than the amount received. The sale of firewood from the woods of West Wycombe brought more money for the lord of the manor, not usually entered in the rent book. In 1779, faggots (bundles of sticks or twigs bound together for fuel) sold at 15s per 100 and brought in £116 16s 3d and 299 loads of thicker firewood brought in £294 17s 6d. Sales in 1775 to the naval dockyard at Chatham of hundreds of loads of oak and elm 'in every respect fitting for His Majesty's Service', brought more profit to Sir Francis and work for the craftsmen and labourers of West Wycombe. Suitable elm wood went to make the *keel pieces* of the largest warships, which carried 64 guns or more, and fought the French navy later in the century.

People of a parish expected the lord of the manor to help needy and worthy causes from his own purse. (A parish with its church often had the same area and boundaries as a manor.) Sir Francis Dashwood did more than just pay poor rate and an annual £5 for bread for the poor. In 1747 he introduced a Bill into the House of Commons to help the unemployed and three years later employed the poor of West Wycombe to build a new and straighter road to High Wycombe, and to enlarge his park. A stone column at the east end of the village, called The Pedestal, marks its completion.

An entry in Thomas Phillibrown's diary for Thursday, 5th October, 1752 says:

> Sir Francis is also making thro' his own grounds, a good new broad road by the side of his park to High Wycombe and the old road which is a low, narrow, washy way, he intends to take into his own park. The Commissioners of the road for this piece of public service are to allow him £10 per annum for 3 years though it is said twill cost him £100 to finish and was it not for the obstinacy

of an ill natured old woman, who would not part with a piece of her field on any terms (to complete so useful a work) Sir Francis would have widened and made good half the road from West to High Wycombe. Sir Francis has a very great character both at High and West Wycombe for a public spirited and a generous man.

The pick-marked cave which runs for a quarter of a mile into West Wycombe hill may be seen as a symbol of Sir Francis Dashwood's public spirit; it is also something of a mystery. Why did he have the men of the village hack out the passages? Was it only to give work to the unemployed? Was it merely to obtain chalk and flints for the new road? Or, were there other ideas at the back of his mind as, down the years, villagers have hinted; for about the caves there have been hints and gossip as about Medmenham Abbey. On the map of 1767 a drawing of a church marks the position of the cave. To this day there stands at the entrance to the cave, a folly which Dashwood built, the front of a church, with pointed arches, walls of flint and an *obelisk*. If you go to West Wycombe you can see these things and walk the quarter of a mile into the cave.

In 1754 the baronet leased 'a *tenement* and cottage, orchard and garden' at Wheeler End, nearly two miles from West Wycombe village, 'for a house or workhouse for the use of the poor of West Wycombe to work and dwell therein and not otherwise'. You can see a photograph of the workhouse as it is today on p. 62. The rent for this was one shilling a year. Sir Francis may have done this with a genuine wish to help the poor, or in order to keep the poor rate low and to move the poor people away from his park gate at one end of the village.

The churchwardens of West Wycombe tried to repair the church from the church rate, paying out, for example, for 'mending ye Church windows and Leads on ye Steeple'. But the church got more and more tumbledown until at last Sir
Francis agreed to rebuild it and make it warmer if the people

of the parish would promise to keep it in good order and not to bury any more dead inside. As in his house, he copied Greek and Roman buildings and employed Italians to paint the ceilings. The interior of the nave, the main part of the church, is a large room or hall with sixteen rich columns against the walls. Both the nave and the chancel, the part of the church where the altar and *communion rails* are, have beautiful marble floors. There is no pulpit or reading desk but instead attractive armchairs on platforms. The *font* is not of stone but is a small bowl on a *tripod* with doves and a serpent for decoration. Visitors today may see these things for themselves, in the church now well preserved and again used for services.

JUSTICE OF THE PEACE

At the age of thirty-eight Sir Francis Dashwood was made a Justice of the Peace, a magistrate for Buckinghamshire. Justices of the Peace had, first of all, to keep the King's Peace, that is to maintain law and order. When two or three magistrates met to try not very important local cases, they met in Petty Sessions. Justices of the Peace also attended Quarter Sessions which were for the county and held four times a year as the name suggests. The Justices in Quarter Sessions tried more serious criminal cases or settled problems of importance to the whole county. Justices of the Peace had to make sure that shopkeepers and others obeyed laws about weights and measures, and that the men of each parish repaired roads and bridges; they licensed *higglers, drovers* and alehouses; they had to keep an eye upon gaols and *houses of correction,* upon some prices, upon the funds for maimed soldiers and upon the way in which overseers of the poor did their work. A Justice of the Peace who did his duty was a very busy man. Many of the squires who could not afford to be Members of Parliament had to be content to be Justices of the Peace. Sir Francis Dashwood was both.

COLONEL OF MILITIA

From 1757 each parish had to send men to become soldiers

Soldiers of a county militia in the eighteenth century

in the county *militia*. In every parish, men chosen by lot for this unpopular service had to serve for three years or pay £10 for a substitute. Small land-owners could pay a rate, as in West Wycombe in 1762, to avoid the risk of having to become a militiaman. For two or three years Sir Francis Dashwood was the commanding officer of the Buckinghamshire militia, with the rank of colonel.

LORD-LIEUTENANT OF BUCKINGHAMSHIRE

Soon after Sir Francis Dashwood had become Lord le Despencer, King George III gave him another honour by appointing him Lord-Lieutenant of Buckinghamshire, which he remained for the rest of his life. Organising the county soldiers or militia and naming the men who were to be made Justices of the Peace were among the duties he had to perform. As Lord-Lieutenant he was the top man in the county, the leader in all that was going on. So it is not surprising to find him arranging great occasions, like this one which was announced in 'St James's Chronicle' or 'British Evening Post' on Thursday, 12 September 1771:

Next Saturday some of the principal Cooks in London

will go to West Wycombe, in Buckinghamshire, being engaged to Dress three Dinners at the Seat of Lord le Despencer; the first next Monday; the second on Wednesday, and the third on Friday; 1,500 Cards of Invitation have been sent to the Nobility, &c. 500 for each Day. A Sacred Oratorio is to be performed at the new Church built by his Lordship.

These festivities may have been part of the celebrations to mark the dedication of the west portico of the mansion house which you read about in the first chapter.

What excitement there must have been in the village! Each travelling coach and four horses, each *chaise* and pair added to the lively and gay scene. With the nobleman and gentry came servants, some in bright colourful *livery*, the number varying with the rank of the guests: personal servants like *valet* and lady's maid; coachman, *groom* and *postilion*, necessary for the journey. All had to be fed. Roads were jammed with vehicles and horses. Alehouse keepers and shopkeepers were hard pressed to serve the extra customers. There was much for the idler to see, and much to take the attention of the labourer or craftsman as he worked. Perhaps it meant a little extra food for all. Even the poor at the park gate may have had a tasty morsel to which they were not accustomed, for the richer the food, the tastier the leavings.

3   Other People in the Parish

When we begin to think about all the other people in the parish besides Sir Francis and Lady Dashwood, we have to help us, 'An Account of All the people in the parish of West Wycombe in 1760', the registers of baptisms, marriages and burials, the accounts of the churchwardens and of the overseers of the poor, many deeds of various kinds, a list of all males between the ages of fifteen and sixty and their occupations in 1798, and two maps made in 1767, one of the manor mentioned at the beginning of the book and one of the Towne (village) opposite. From these we can tell how many there were in each household, how the household was made up, whether the householder lived alone, whether the householder, if a man, had a wife, children or other relatives living with him and how many, if any, servants he kept. It is sometimes even possible to point to a house and to say who were living there in the 1760s.

Some of the villagers like Widow Ing, Widow Keene, Charles Fletcher and the unnamed Officer of Excise lived alone. James Edsell, who also lived alone would not lack visitors for his was the village barber's shop. For others the problem was overcrowding. In a house at Booker lived William and John Tilbury, their wives, two children, a mother with four children and a servant. Although in the eighteenth century many babies died at birth or when they were very young, some families had to find food for as many as eight hungry children. This was the number that William Childs and his

35

A poor woman and her five children

wife had to feed and clothe. John Ford and his wife had seven, and five other families had six children each. At Mill End Farm lived John Boddy, *yeoman*, with his wife, two children and eight servants, some of whom were probably not domestic servants but farm-hands, or other workpeople living with the family. Another farmer, Aaron Wooster—he had difficulty in writing his name and spelling it correctly—occupied Chawley Farm with his wife, six children and three servants. The account of all the people in West Wycombe in 1760 begins with Sir Francis and Lady Dashwood who had no children, and ends with 'Workhouse Family 27'.

The count of the population of the village in 1760 did not include *vagrants*, passing through the village. In fact poor people from other parishes were unwelcome and were not allowed to stay if discovered. The reason for this was that an Act of Parliament passed in 1667 had said that any person settling in a parish might be removed at once unless he rented a house or cottage worth £10 or more. Poor people were not allowed to stay for fear that they would ask for money from the poor rate. They were expected to go to the parish to which they belonged, usually where they were born. Some vagrants reached West Wycombe but went no further, as entries in the burial registers show:

> Matthew Youstrise a poor travelor that dyed upon Wheler end (Wheeler End) common.
> A Travailing woman found dead in a barn.
> A child dy'd in a Barn, it's name unknown.
> A man killed by a Waggon Name unknown.
> Infant Gipsy drown'd.

William Bishop was luckier. He was a labourer who had been

born in West Wycombe, and he had to make his way back there with his child. You can see above a copy of a certificate given to him. He had to make his way from St Giles in the Fields in London and 'peaceably and quietly to pass to West Wycombe that being their legal settlement'. Written at the side of the certificate are the amounts allowed them in *relief* and assistance in the parishes through which they passed:

A person wishing to move from his own parish for work had to take with him a Certificate of Settlement signed by the churchwardens and overseers of the poor of his parish. They had to be ready to receive him again if he claimed money from the poor rate. Without his certificate he would not be allowed to stay in the new parish.

Overseers of the poor in West Wycombe and other parishes could be brutal to a woman without a husband. In the neighbouring parish of High Wycombe Lord Shelburne advised the parish officers when told of a 'travelling woman as lay sick with a feather [fever] with 4 children in Ye Lord Shelburns Brick Kilns' to give her money (2s 6d) and send her away. In West Wycombe the churchwardens on occasion gave 1s to 'a great bellied woman to go forward'.

LABOURING POOR

Of the 250 men between the ages of fifteen and sixty in West Wycombe in 1798, 141 are described as labourers. In England and Wales in the eighteenth century more than half the population in the countryside did not earn enough to pay for the bare necessities of food, clothes and a roof over their heads. These were the labouring poor, cottagers living in small cottages or hovels with little or no land, workers in the fields who were not employed regularly by farmers, the sick and the old, and men in work whose wages were not enough to support their wives and families. To make up the difference between earnings and needs they could beg, they could ask the churchwardens and the overseers of the poor for help, at harvest they could *glean* in the fields, they could steal, they could poach fish from the stream or rabbits, hares, doves, pheasants and the occasional deer.

38   A labourer could earn about one shilling a day. In 1720

Most people worked on the land as farm labourers

when a strong wind blew tiles from the roof of West Wycombe church, the churchwardens paid Thomas Wheeler 5s for three days and his man 3s, and together they were given sixpence for beer. Workmen often received beer money in this way. Churchwardens paid for beer for the bellringers when they rang the bells of the church of St Lawrence on the hill on the anniversary of the Gunpowder Plot, the King's or Queen's birthday or at the news of an important event. One of the chief expenses at a pauper's funeral was beer. For the funeral of 'Richard Harris boy' the coffin cost 6s 6d and beer (safer to drink than unboiled water) 2s 6d—perhaps instead of wages for grave-digger and bearer.

An unemployed or poorly paid labourer could always make 39

A vermin catcher carrying his traps

a little honest money by hunting and killing the vermin which infested the lands of the manor, and attacked the domestic fowl and their eggs, the pheasants and ornamental birds, the fish in the lake and mill-brook. There were red-furred, bushy-tailed foxes, small dark-brown evil smelling polecats, the insect-eating hedgehogs (probably harmless), and the grey-coated badgers, hunters of fish by night. The churchwardens paid one shilling each for foxes and badgers, fourpence for polecats, and twopence for hedgehogs. Polecats were the most numerous. Payments for badgers were seldom made.

One of the vicars of West Wycombe wrote at the front of his account book how much he paid his servants. Harris, was to have £18 a year and a load of wood; John Revening received £9 a year and Thomas Bache £8 'if he behaved well, if not £7.7s'. The last two lived with the vicar, so they had free food and lodging; Revening was also allowed £1 a year for leather breeches.

What did the labouring families eat? Most of the time they lived on bread. They could buy a halfpenny, a penny or a twopenny loaf but the weights of these loaves varied with the price of corn, and that depended on the previous harvest. On the other hand they could buy a loaf of fixed weight, the price of which would go up and down with the price of corn. The half peck loaf, 8lb 11oz (4kg) in weight, was popular and normally would cost one shilling—a day's wage. Bad harvests meant less to eat. Inside the cover of the burial register of West Wycombe are written the ominous words— 'The Winter of 1708 was a very cold hard winter ye summer following was a dear year of corn'. From another source, we learn that:

> 7th Jan very severe frost began this day and lasted 3 months, a very hard frost for a long tyme besides and all things very dere so that a half penny rowle weighed just a crown piece [5s] and two turnips sold for a penny and coals sold for 40s a quarter.

At various times during the eighteenth century there were years of poor harvest. In 1794 West Wycombe Vestry asked for gifts of money so that the poor could still buy their half peck loaf for one shilling. The workhouse accounts towards the end of the century tell us the prices of other foods besides bread. Beef cost from 3½d to 5½d per lb, mutton from 3d to 6d, cheese 4½d or 5d pork 6d and bacon 8½d. From another source we know that a quarter of a pound of tea (a delicacy in those days) cost one shilling, a pound of sugar 6d, and a pound of butter 6d or 7d.

The poor needed clothes as well as food, and the accounts of the churchwardens and the overseers of the poor tell us how much they provided; for example, a hat and breeches for John Phillips, a pair of breeches and a pair of shoes for Putman's boy; a shirt for a pauper boy and an apron and *shifts* for his sister, two pairs of stockings for Fryer's boy, and a shirt and shift for Besley and his wife. They paid 6s 6d for one chair, about a week's wages of a labourer, but another, for Widow Toovey, cost only 2s 6d.

YEOMEN, FARMERS, THE VICAR, THE PARISH CLERK: WHO WAS THEN A GENTLEMAN?

In the record of all the people in West Wycombe in 1760, Sir Francis and Lady Dashwood head the list. Following them is a group of twenty-five men all of whom have 'Mr' written before their names and one woman, Mrs Hurls. Of the rest only the vicar and three papermakers are called Mr. For the others only Christian names and surnames are given. Women whose husbands had died before the count was made are entered as widows like Widow Keene or Widow Gray, but some are called Mrs Besides, Mrs Hurls, there are Mrs Browne, probably the widow of a previous vicar, Mrs Burdett who lived with her, Mrs Barnabee, Mrs Bailey and a few others.

The use of Mr or Mrs before a name seems to mean a person important in the life of the village and parish or a person high in the local social scale. First among the men entered after Sir Francis and Lady Dashwood is Thomas Dorrell, Mr here but esquire in another document. He had two servants and he lived in a house overlooking the park of Sir Francis. He owned in one part of 'the Towne' a house and two gardens and in another at least thirteen cottages, a slaughterhouse, a barn, yards, an orchard and gardens, be-

A farmyard and farmhouse of the time

sides lands in other parts of the parish.

The rest of the leading group of twenty-six seem to have been farmers. Twenty-three of the twenty-six had servants living with them, sixty-six servants in all. Mrs Hurls held a farm: as you read in Chapter 2 she paid rent to the lord of the manor for it. Her husband had died in 1759, as their gravestone to the south of the church on the hill tells us. The husband of Mrs Barrabee, another widow is described in some deeds as yeoman and in another as gentleman. The social ranks appear to have been gentleman, yeoman, farmer, *husbandman* and labourer (in that order), but it is not clear just how one differed from the rest. Mrs Bailey is shown on the map of West Wycombe in 1767 as owner of houses, cottages, a malthouse, gardens and an orchard. As such she would be looked upon as an important person in the village.

The Reverend Richard Levett was vicar of West Wycombe

The gravestone of Richard and Anne Hurls. The writing at the bottom says: 'Happy they liv'd for Probity rever'd Mankind they lov'd their GOD they also fear'd Tho' parted long they are met again to prove Friendship immortal everlasting love.' What is the meaning of 'Probity'?

from 1765 to 1805. He was also Rector of Halton a few miles from West Wycombe and as he could not be in both parishes at once, he had to pay a *curate* to do the work in one parish for him. He probably travelled on horseback as there is mention of a black mare and a new saddle but no mention of a carriage. The lord of the manor chose the vicars. The vicar chose the *parish clerk*. The village allowed the clerk 10s a year and every householder gave him fourpence. A note on the inside cover of the vicar's account book reads: 'William Winter Lawrance began his clerkship on April 19th in the year 1752.'

In Chapter 2 you read about Lawrance as receiver employed by the lord of the manor and keeping the massive rent book. From his style of writing we can see that he made the account of all the people in West Wycombe in 1760. He may have made it so that he could be sure that he received the fourpence from every house due to him, or he may have made it to be sure that there was no poor person in the parish who should be moved on. When a wedding took place William Winter Lawrance was there to witness the signature or mark of bride and bridegroom. He also wrote the minutes of vestry meetings and kept account of money received and paid out by the churchwardens and the overseers of the poor. A very useful man to have in the village!

CRAFTSMEN, TRADERS: THE MIDDLING SORT

William Winter Lawrance, parish clerk, lived in a house in the centre of the village. The village had two streets, the main street, called High Street, and Church Lane running at right-angles northward towards the church on the hill. His house was one of a row on the north side of High Street, six doors from the junction with Church Lane. From here, by sight, sound and sometimes by smell, he could tell what was happening in the village.

With a malthouse at each end of the village the parish clerk would be well aware that maltmaking was an important occupation in West Wycombe. The maltsters made more malt than the parish required and sent quantities by road to the

Barges carried cargo and were pulled by horses in the eighteenth century

River Thames at Great Marlow. Barges, often with names like the 'King's Arms', the 'Ship of Henley', the 'Dove' or the 'Angel', carried the malt from Marlow to London. The journey was sometimes dangerous as the barges had to shoot the weirs on the river through *flash locks*. Tax had to be paid on malt before it left Marlow and when a barge met with an accident and sank, the maltsters were quick to ask for a refund of tax already paid on the malt lost and the Collector of Excise was called in. In 1723 William Davenport, matter of West Wycombe received a refund of tax when a load of malt sank in the River Thames. The sale in one year of nearly 3,500 hop poles by the lord of the manor suggests that many hops were grown as well as much malt made and beer brewed in West Wycombe itself. (On pages 51–54, you can read a detailed description of beer-making in the eighteenth century.)

From William Lawrance's house he might hear the lowing of cows, the bleating of sheep or the neighing of horses from the pound which was enclosed ground, at the west end of the 45

A blacksmith's shop

village into which they had been driven or led when they had strayed. There they would stay until their owner claimed them. Between the Black Boy Inn and the Swan alehouse stood Mr Dorrell's slaughterhouse. From the hides of the cattle the cordwainers (shoemakers) made shoes.

As in all villages, there were in West Wycombe craftsmen on whom the farmers depended: blacksmiths, wheelwrights or wheelers, carpenters, brick and tile makers and brick-layers. The smith's shop and dwelling house of James Noble was next door to the parish clerk's house and there were eight blacksmiths in the parish. There were three wheelers to repair the ninety-two wagons and carts in the parish and attend to wagons, chaises and coaches if they broke down as they passed through. One, Abraham Mead had his shop in Church Lane. There were nine carpenters. The craftsmen in brick and tile worked where brick-earth and suitable clay could be found. The kilns (ovens) in which bricks were baked are marked on the map of 1767, and hollows in the earth still show where they were.

Perhaps the most interesting workers in wood were the turners. A turner used a simple but effective pole *lathe*. The

Before the hides of cattle could be used by the cordwainer for making shoes, they had to be tanned. Here is a tanner at work

A wheelwright

A turner using a pole and treadle lathe

The brick-maker. Notice the mould into which he will put the soft clay

force to drive it came from the turner's leg muscles as they worked the treadle, the springiness in a long slender pole returning the *treadle* to its original position. With pole lathes turners could make bowls, wooden pots, lace bobbins, legs and stretchers for chairs, legs for stools including milking stools and even toys and games. Turners and others began to specialise in the making of chairs. John Harris, mentioned in 1762 as having·a turner's shop, ten years later was a chairmaker. Abraham Mead was both wheelwright and chairmaker. By 1800 there were nearly twenty chairmakers.

As the parish clerk walked through the village, along the lanes and roads of the parish, he would see women and girls sitting in doors and windows making pillow lace sometimes called bobbin or bone lace. The pillows on which they worked the lace, were square or round, made of canvas, resting on a stand called a pillow horse or a pillow maid. The lace-makers needed pins of various styles, some with ornamented heads, thread of cotton or flax, and bobbins usually of bone

The bobbins and pillow of a lace-maker, resting on a pillow horse or maid

or wood. Lace merchants like Samuel and Thomas Johnson or Joseph Pontifix went round the parish giving out thread to the lace-makers and often patterns and receiving the finished lace for sale in London. Even young children might work for four or five hours a day, and women as many as twelve or fifteen. Although working long hours they earned perhaps eightpence or tenpence a day, rather less than a labourer's wage. But the money received from lace-making helped to buy food and clothes necessary to keep the family alive.

If the parish clerk took his walk along the main road about half-a-mile towards High Wycombe, he would hear the sound of water-wheels turned by the stream called the mill-brook. As he drew nearer he would see that there were three mills some distance apart as there had been when King William I's scribes had long ago recorded details of the manor for Domesday Book. It is not surprising that that part of the parish was called Mill End. In the eighteenth century they were paper mills, but it seems that one mill not only worked hammers, which beat rags into pulp for paper, but also ground corn into flour. In one of the mills Edmund Ball made white paper

A mill driven by water from a stream

*A baker kneading dough.
Behind him is the oven
in which he baked his bread*

and put a finish on it which none of the other numerous mills on the stream could produce. In parishes where there was not a large enough stream, windmills ground the corn and in parts of the country where coal was mined stationary steam engines pumped water from the pits. But in many parts, apart from muscles of men and horses, water-wheels and windmills were the chief sources of power.

Besides these craftsmen, West Wycombe had a small number of shopkeepers, bakers, tailors and the occasional glover, potter, collar-maker, heel-maker, tanner and other craftsmen. The lord of the manor had his steward, his gamekeeper, his wood-man and his servants. If we need a name to cover all the various people described in this chapter who were not gentle-men and not labouring poor, perhaps the best is the one used in the eighteenth century—'the middling sort'. Most of the craftsmen used products of the farms and woods of the parish, but lace-making used thread and paper-making used rags— both brought from outside the parish. Malt, corn, timber (particularly beech in various forms), chairs and lace found markets elsewhere, especially in London, transported by road or by the River Thames.

Bad luck could soon turn a craftsman into a *pauper*. James Cox, a glover, in 1711 'by reason of lameness in his right hand occasioned by the dread *palsy* and his eyesight much decayed, and having several running sores in his legs' was not able to provide for himself, his wife and eight children. When the officers of the parish failed to move him and his family to Bicester in Oxfordshire (where he was born), and gave him 7s 6d weekly, afterwards reduced to 5s, inhabitants of West Wycombe complained to the Justices of the Peace that he was still paid too much!

MAKING BEER

You have read earlier in this chapter about beer given to workmen as wages or in addition to wages, of beer for bell-ringers and beer at funerals. You will see on the map of the village on page 35 the names of eight inns and alehouses along the main street. As in other villages and towns people drank much beer. The first stage in the making was the turning of barley, sometimes oats or wheat, into malt and the second stage the brewing of the beer. The map shows a malthouse at each end of the village and you have read about William Davenport maltster of West Wycombe.

The process which was needed to make the barley into malt changed the starch in the barley into a kind of sugar necessary to provide alcohol for the beer. To do this the maltster steeped the barley in water, making the grain swell and become soft. He then spread it out on the malting floor in a thick and even layer called the Couch: the grain smelt a bit like apples and was warm and moist. Because of the heat which built up, the grain started to germinate. When rootlets appeared, the maltster spread the grain more thinly to reduce the heat. He would continue to do this, called flooring, for about fourteen days. The illustration on the next page shows this process. The starch in the grain was now on the way to being changed into sugar.

Another picture shows how the maltster dried the grain in 51

Steeping, couching and flooring malt

The cooler

52 *The malt kiln* *A vat for storing beer*

An eighteenth-century brewhouse, showing the different processes involved

a kiln, spreading it out with wooden shovels and forks on a floor with holes, which allowed the heat to come through from the furnace below. After he had left the grain to cool, he pressed it through shoots, causing the roots formed during germination to fall off. The grain fell through the shoots onto a wire screen and the maltster spread it out, leaving it until it was soft. The grain had become malt ready for brewing.

You will read in Chapter 5 how we know that the vicarage, the Swan inn and a house nearby, each had a brewhouse and it is likely that there were others in the village. Although domestic brewhouses and those of village inns were probably smaller and simpler than the one shown on this page, the processes were much the same. In West Wycombe the brewers would heat the copper with wood or charcoal. Six processes were needed to brew the beer. In the illustration you can see the copper (A) and the furnace (C) which heated the water. 53

The brewer ground the malt and mixed it with hot water in the mash tun (D) just below the copper, stirring with long poles called oars (E). Having done this several times to dissolve the sugar in the malt, he strained the liquid, called sweet wort into the copper, boiling it with hops to give taste and keep it in good condition. Then the brewer moved the liquid into a cooler (H) and, when it had cooled, into a vat or tun, where he added yeast to make it ferment, turning sugar into alcohol and the liquid into beer. When all the bits of grain had gradually sunk to the bottom, the brewer could draw off the clear beer into storage vats or casks for drinking or selling.

4 Parish Affairs and Officers

Among the parish records of West Wycombe is a book, bound in parchment, with brown lettering on the front cover telling us that it was WEST WYCOMBE VESTERY BOOK. It contains a record, called minutes, of meetings of inhabitants of the parish from 1744 to 1809. Other books contain minutes of parish meetings before 1744 and after 1809.

The parish people meeting in this way to make decisions about parish affairs, were called the vestry. Each parish had had its vestry for two or three hundred years before the eighteenth century. If all those who paid parish rates had come, between 120 and 150 would have been there. But sometimes there were as few as four. In 1760–61 the number varied between seven and fifteen. Twenty-five attended one or more of the five meetings of the vestry during the year. Four, James Turner, Thomas Batting, John Boddy and Aaron Wooster, all yeoman farmers, were present at all the meetings. Others who came were farmers, three papermakers, a shopkeeper, an innkeeper, a *victualler*, a butcher, the parish clerk and Thomas Dorrell, esquire. In July 1754 the vestry established a parish workhouse under the care of Thomas Deane. At the vestry meeting which decided to give Deane £270 a year to maintain the poor, twenty-two inhabitants were present, including Sir Francis Dashwood, lord of the manor, and Rev. Ed. Brown, vicar.

In many parishes the vestry met in the parish church but at West Wycombe the church stood on the top of the hill a distance from the village and two hundred feet above it. 55

Once or twice the vestry met in the church but usually in a building on the north side of High Street called the Church Loft. It is described in Chapter 5. Sometimes the vestry met in the George Inn or the Black Boy Inn, but in 1762 it was decided that 'for the future all business shall be done in the Church or Loft and the books shall never be carried into a Public House'.

At Easter the vestry appointed two churchwardens. At other times the vestry appointed overseers of the poor, constables, and the surveyor of the highways, or they named several men from whom Justices of the Peace made a choice. The vestry decided when the 'inhabitants and occupiers of lands' should pay church rate and poor rate, and how much the rate should be.

The care of the poor was the churchwardens' biggest problem and the inhabitants had to pay much more in poor rate than in church rate, and had to pay it more often. In 1716 the vestry decided that the poor who received help from the parish must each wear a badge, 'and not a penny to be paid to any person that shall be seen without a badge or refuse to wear the same'. By law the badge was to be a large Roman P made of red or blue cloth and worn on the shoulder of the right sleeve.

Often vestry minutes read, 'It was agreed to Consider about the Poor', and give a list of requests from the poor usually for clothes, or for firewood or coal. On the left hand side of the page either 'Allowed' (sometimes spelt 'aloud'), or 'No' is written. If the item was allowed, as it usually was, the name of the shopkeeper who was to supply is often written on the right—Shanks, Gadbury, Irving, Grange or Russell.

> *Allowed* Widow Jones Some Coals
> John Lane Some Wood   Mr Keen
> Joseph Ing a pair of Breaches   Grange
> Ed Deans boy a hatt and pr of stockings ye Gairl (girl) a peticoate
> agreed for Mary Graing to mend Thomas Eastes Brechis (breeches)

                    the other girls Stays to be mended   Henry
                    Shanks
No   John Stiles a coat
                    Thos Richards a Wascoat (waistcoat)
                    Lady Bisly a Shift.

After the vestry had appointed Thomas Deane governor of
the workhouse the poor came under his care and the minutes
no longer include items allowed to them.

THE CHURCHWARDENS

Churchwardens had many things to do. Three times a year
the *archdeacon* came round. In the churchwardens' accounts
for West Wycombe, expenses appear for the attendance of the
churchwardens on the archdeacon, or even the bishop, who
might be visiting another parish like Amersham, Beaconsfield
or Great Marlow several miles away. About Easter, soon after
the churchwardens had been appointed, they had to be present
at the visitation to be sworn in. At the two other visitations
churchwardens had to hand in copies of the entries in
the parish registers of baptisms, marriages and burials.
The churchwardens had a duty to report to the archdeacon's
court anything that was wrong or disorderly in the parish
such as drunkenness, swearing, disturbing divine service or
not attending church on Sundays and holy days.

Churchwardens had to provide bread and wine for *communion*. In 1717 they paid Sir Francis Dashwood 11*s* for wine
'for ye Communion Several Times' but a more usual entry
was 'Paid to Mary Gray for Bread for the Communion. 8*d*;
Paid Mrs Jennings (George Inn) for Wine for the Communion
£1 4*s*'. Not more than once every three years the churchwardens
paid men to 'beat the bounds' to make sure that parish boundaries were as they should be. Sometimes money had to be
spent on the churchyard hedge.

Bell ringing on special anniversaries, at the churchwardens'
expense in wages or beer, went on throughout the century.
In 1705 the bells rang out on the anniversary of 'ye Gunpowder-
treason day', on 'ye Queens (Queen Anne) Birth day' and 'ye   57

Queens Coronation Day', 'for Newes of a Victory obtained by the Duke of Marlborough', and on 'Ye Thanksgiving-Day appointed for the late Victory'. By 1766 the bells rang the King's birthday, the Coronation Day and 'powder Plott'.

The money to pay the churchwardens' expenses came from the church rate. The amount of the rate could vary from time to time. The names of all those who paid the rate were recorded, and how much they paid, and lastly the items on which the churchwardens had spent money and the cost of each. Payments for repairs to the church and cleaning the church often appeared. These are some of the items:

> a Buckett and a Tubb to use at ye Church
> for mending y church windows and Leads on ye Steeple
> cleaning the rubbish out of the tower and brooms
> a *Turk's Head* to take the Cobwebs Downe
> for getting snow out of the Sceeling
> James Noble for Carriage of the Bell
> for Casting the fifth Bell
> for getting the Bell up the Steeple and Hanging

Sometimes the churchwardens gave money to poor travellers:

> a New England merchant with a letter of request with a wife and 12 children
> a disbanded solger [soldier] with a wife and 4 children
> two familys which lost their goods by ye sea breaking out upon them.

The churchwardens paid for the upkeep of the village clock, the village *stocks* and the bridges across the stream which ran through village and parish. The clock was not in the tower of the church on the hill where it would not be seen by the villagers, but in the village itself where it projected into the main street. In 1713–14 Joseph Delafield was paid £1 'for keeping the clock for one year'; and in 1768–69 the same. sum was paid to James Noble 'for winding up the clock'. The churchwardens in 1764-65 John Martin and William Hunt had new stocks built.

Two offenders in the stocks

The village stocks in which people who had broken the law in a small way had to sit with their legs locked, the whipping post, the lock-up and the clock were all close together. In fact, the chains of the clock hung down into the lock-up, and there is a story of an offender who, put in the lock-up for the night by the parish constable, escaped by climbing up the chains, causing the clock to tick rapidly and earning for himself the name of 'Ticky' Biggs.

Bridges crossed the stream at various points and a *causeway* ran through the village. Between 1702 and 1739 the church-wardens paid

    'for stones and Gravell to repair the Causey'
    'for Mending the Church yrd Gate and the Bridge nigh
     Jos Burnham's house'

'for clearing the river under the bridge house'
and 'for building the bridge at Mill End'.

When the churchwardens reached the end of their year of office they had to show their accounts to the vestry meeting. At the end of the accounts the words 'remain in purs' or 'out of purse' or 'out of pockett' were written and often some such phrases as 'seen and allowed by us', the signatures of all those present or, if they could not write their names, their mark.

Churchwardens in the village were usually farmers. A man chosen to be churchwarden could be heavily fined if he refused. Men might serve for one year only and be glad when their year of office came to an end. Others may have felt important as churchwarden and enjoyed the dignity of sharing the most important position in the parish. Richard Barrabee and Robert Lavell were churchwardens in West Wycombe for three years 1713–15. Between 1760 and 1777 William Hunt was churchwarden thirteen times and between 1781 and 1795 William Cubbage variously described as baker, paper-maker, shopkeeper and farmer held the office six times. From 1790 to 1800 only six men were churchwardens. Of these John Martin and John Wooster, both farmers, were churchwardens together for five successive years. Two others were farmers and Thomas Francis was a miller. Farmers had much power in the village.

PARISH OFFICERS: OVERSEERS OF THE POOR

An important Act of Parliament passed in 1601 ordered that in each parish the churchwardens and four, three or two substantial householders should be nominated each year as overseers of the poor. They were to maintain and set to work the poor with funds provided by the rate for relief of the poor. The men chosen by the vestry to be overseers had to take the office whether they wanted it or not; they were untrained and usually, but not always, unpaid; a few could not write. The poor rate in West Wycombe brought in £115 in 1714 and £465 in 1799. The overseers had to look after the sick and pauper children, and find food for the hungry, homes for the homeless, clothes and shoes for those who were dressed only in rags and were bare-footed, and work for those who could work but couldn't get any.

The overseers of the poor entered in their parchment-bound book the amount paid by each ratepayer. Sir Francis Dashwood, heading the list as the squire, had the most to pay. After the amounts received came the payments made to or for the poor. Money was paid out to help people in various ways. These are only a few of the many entries: it was given for 'being sick', 'being hurt with a cart', 'to go for a cure for his wife's eyes, she being blind', 'being out of work', mending shoes, firewood, 'keeping two travillers, one having the smallpox', to a widow, three of her family having smallpox, for 'an apron, *bib and strings*, and a bodis [bodice] coat'.

There were several ways in which the overseers provided homes for the poor. At Lane End, a remote *hamlet* in the parish, there were four parish houses, in which paupers were allowed to live. The room below the church loft was divided into tenements which were let. Rent was paid for some dozen of the poor, at least half of them widows. Others were boarded out, sometimes with other paupers.

Perhaps the most difficult task which the overseers had to face was how to provide work for those who were able to work but hadn't a job. As you have read in Chapter 2, West Wycombe set up a workhouse about a mile and a half from the village on the edge of Wheeler End Common. Here Thomas Deane was responsible for all the poor of the parish, keeping, clothing and employing some and paying all weekly allowances and other reliefs out of the £270 per annum paid to him by monthly instalments. The workhouse is still there, with the name on the gate—The Old Workhouse. Now it is a private house, but it still has a wooden grille through which the governor could look to see how the paupers were working and behaving.

In 1757 the vestry decided that 'the persons that dyeth out of the Workhouse that cannot bury themselves he shall burry them and shall not have their clothes'. This probably meant that if a poor person, not someone who lived in the workhouse, 61

A photograph of the eighteenth-century workhouse in West Wycombe as it looks today

had not enough money when he died to pay for his own funeral, the governor of the workhouse had to pay for the coffin, and the wool that must go in it, from the money he was paid each month. He was not allowed to have the pauper's clothes for his own use or to sell them. By the end of the century the workhouse had been enlarged and there were some ten acres of land on which those capable could work.

Poor boys and girls could be *apprenticed* by the churchwardens and overseers of the poor. For each child apprenticed a document called an indenture of apprenticeship had to be signed by two justices of the peace. We still have thirty of these from West Wycombe, all of them from the eighteenth century. The person with whom a child was placed had to promise to take him or her for a stated number of years and to 'provide and allow unto the said Apprentice, *meet*, competent, and sufficient Meat, Drink, and Apparel, Lodging, Washing and other things necessary and fit for an Apprentice' and to teach the apprentice or cause him or her to be instructed in the best manner he could in the art or trade named in the indenture. When, in 1732, Henry Shanks of West Wycombe, tailor, took Jane Oxlade as an apprentice for seven years (not for tailoring but in housewifery), he received £4 4s from churchwardens and overseers of the poor: the usual sum was round about £5.

Among the thirty apprenticeships in West Wycombe which we know about, the length of the apprenticeship varied from four years to nine or until the apprentice had reached the age of twenty-four, twenty-one or twenty. Housewifery was the 'art or mystery' in eight of the apprenticeships and husbandry in three. Three blacksmiths took apprentices, three paper-makers, two glovers, two mantuamakers (dressmakers), two cordwainers (shoemakers), one sawyer or carpenter, one shovelmaker, one miller, one tailor, one baker, and a tin plate worker. Some of the apprentices were given genuine training. William Bradford taken by Richard Robinson as an apprentice in 1716 for the trade of blacksmith, himself took Robert Oxlade as an apprentice blacksmith 63 in 1731. At the end of the apprenticeship the master normally had to give the apprentice 'double Apparell of all sorts, good and new (that is to say) a good new Suit, for the Holy-days and another for Working days'.

CONSTABLE AND TITHINGMEN

The odd job man in the parish was the constable. His true name was the petty constable as distinct from the high or chief constable. The high constable was responsible for a group of parishes known as a hundred. West Wycombe was in the Hundred of Desborough. The County of Buckinghamshire was at that time divided into eight *hundreds*. In some parishes the petty constable was called a tithingman or sometimes the name tithingman was given to a deputy or assistant constable, as in West Wycombe. These men were not usually farmers. William Bavin, chairmaker and shopkeeper, and Abraham Mead, wheelwright and chairmaker, were constable and tithingman for three years 1791 to 1794. Thomas White was constable for six years with three men each year to help him.

The constable had to arrange for 'watch and ward' to be kept in the parish from dusk to dawn, for the guards to arrest any strangers who appeared and prevent '*homicides*, robberies, thefts, riots, tumults, or other offences.' The constable of the parish was also expected to help with the enlistment of men for the army, as this extract of April 1708 shows: 'James Gardner, brought by the constable of West Wycombe, was handed over to Matthew Hall, Lieutenant in the company of foot under the command of Captain Robert Henington in the regiment of Colonel Roger Elliott.'

The constable, too, had to take to court—the Quarter Sess-ions—offenders against the law. Many offenders were poachers. For example, in 1711 Robert Hawes of West Wycombe, la-bourer, was charged with 'setting snares and killing hares and destroying the game'. Others brought before the court were John Beckley, for killing four doves, and three labourers for fishing in a private fishery and taking away nineteen eels. 64 There were many other offences such as absence from church on four successive Sundays, the exercising of a trade without having served a legal apprenticeship, keeping greyhounds, building cottages on the wasteland without licence, refusing to keep watch and ward, or to labour on the roads, when ordered to do so, attacking the constable himself and sheltering vagrants. There were so many things for the constable to do that it was impossible for him to do them all properly. It is not surprising that constables' reports sometimes said that all was well when all' was not well.

SURVEYOR OF THE HIGHWAYS

The roads of the parish were kept in repair by what was known as statute labour. By law 'every parishioner for every *ploughland* and every person keeping a team of horses or plough, had to provide for four days in the year' 'one wain or cart furnished after the custom of the country and also two able men with the same'. Most other men in the parish had each, either to put in four days labour or to send 'one sufficient labourer in his stead'. This unpaid statute labour was supervised by a surveyor of the highways who also was unpaid. The vestry suggested several men for the office, from whom the Justices of the Peace chose one or two. Three times a year, the surveyor had to report to a justice on the state of the roads in the parish and it was his duty to arrange the times when his fellow parishioners should carry out their unpleasant statute labour and supervise their work. Unpaid, untrained for the work, bullied by the justices and unpopular with the people, many a surveyor must have looked forward to the end of his year in this office. Surveyors of the highways found that, with statute labour, they could not mend the main road through the parish properly. 'Much frequented by Waggons and other heavy carriages', it had become 'very ruinous and out of repair'. In 1719 an Act of Parliament appointed trustees to repair this road, from Stokenchurch to Beaconsfield, allowing them to set up turnpike gates at which road users, except pedestrians, had to pay toll. Money collected paid for repairs and other improvements to the road. 65

5 Homes in the Village

A coach and six. Notice the basket at the back for luggage and passengers

WALLS, ROOFS AND CHIMNEYS

A walk along the village high street today will show the houses and cottages very much as they were in the eighteenth century. The map of West Wycombe in 1767 shows eight inns and alehouses in the high street. Of these the George (now called the George and Dragon) and the Swan are still in business. A third, the Plough in 1973 offers food and drink, but although the date 1727 is cut into a brick at the front, it is not on the 1767 map. The eighteenth-century White Hart, Coach and Horses, Unicorn, Black Boy, Wheel, Lion and Chequers are now private houses or shops. The arches of the George and

66

the Black Boy inns remain and remind us of vehicles and horses which passed under them to stables at the back. The vehicles would be carriages, coaches, *post-chaises* or *phaetons* either privately owned or hired. They would not be *stage-coaches* or *mail-coaches,* as these stopped to change horses in the neighbouring town of High Wycombe. During the last ten years of the century the Birmingham stage-coach passed through West Wycombe on its way to London at about 8.30 in the morning, returning about 9.30 in the evening. Worcester, Gloucester and Oxford coaches made similar journeys to London in the morning and from London in the afternoon or evening. From 1785, the Shrewsbury mail-coaches disturbed the sleeping villagers; the down coach, some thirty miles out of London with another one hundred miles to go, soon after one o'clock in the morning and the up coach two or three hours later.

In the houses along the village street and up Church Lane many of the people you have read about lived and worked, not the farmers, but the vicar, the parish clerk, and craftsmen. Some of their houses were built in the eighteenth century and some were already old when the century began. Little building has been done since the eighteenth century and as the National Trust took over the village in 1934, it is now preserved. Electric light, and main drainage have replaced the *rushlight,* candle, oil lamp and the *'necessary house'* but the buildings, inside and out, are not very different from what they were two hundred years ago.

In West Wycombe there is not a thatched cottage to be seen. There were some thatched cottages in the parish in the eighteenth century but most houses had tiled roofs. Brickmakers baked tiles and bricks together, using clay found in the parish. Thatched roofs easily caught fire but were cheaper than tiles or stone slates. Where walls were not strong enough to carry tiles the roofs had to be of thatch, but in West Wycombe walls were timberframed with infilling, or built of brick or brick and flint, all strong enough to carry tiles. You can still see all these materials in the walls if you walk through the 67 village. Beginning at the west, the Oxford end of the village, you will notice on the right, near the entrance to the park, a long wall of *flint* with some brick. This was the malthouse of William Davenport, for a time chief or head constable of the Hundred of Desborough. He owned a house, five cottages and a garden adjoining the malthouse, and liked to be thought a gentleman. The labourers whose wages he did not pay until ordered to do so by the justices in Quarter Sessions, probably had another name for him. It was he who lost malt in the Thames when the boat carrying it sank. At various times he was overseer of the poor, churchwarden, a trustee of the turnpike road, and as a member of the vestry he was allowed to sign the churchwardens' accounts.

A little further along the village street stood the Swan, dwelling house, brewhouse and stables, and opposite a timber-framed two-storeyed house with the corner wall posts reaching to the eaves, which are still standing. On the north side of the street opposite are three cottages, timber-framed but with overhanging upper storey; these seem to be the cottages which were insured, with three others, by the Sun Fire Office in 1738. The largest, occupied by William Dormer, shopkeeper, was insured for £100. They are all described in the policy as part brick, part timber, part plaster. One was the White Hart Inn on the map of 1767. An overhanging upper storey helped to keep the lower part dry at a time when buildings had no gutters at the eaves and no downpipes. As overhanging upper storeys went out of fashion in the reign of Queen Elizabeth I, these cottages must have been over 100 years old when the eighteenth century began.

Timber-framed houses, sometimes called half-timbered houses, had a skeleton or cage of timbers, while their wall-posts, *studs, tie-beams, joists* and *rafters* were held together by *mortise and tenon joints*, secured with *dowels* cut from the heart of an oak tree. The wooden skeleton was made in a shop or yard and then brought to the place where the house was to stand. There the frame was put together and hoisted into position on a prepared base or plinth of stone, brick, flint or

68

large squared beams of oak laid flat. When the frame was in position the spaces between the studs (upright timbers) had to be filled. The earliest kind of infilling was *wattle* and *daub*. Lengths of oak, beech or chestnut were split into flat strips and fitted horizontally or vertically into grooves and then fixed with nails. Sometimes twigs were interwoven, making a basketwork called wattle. The builder covered the wattle with daub, made of wet clay or mud mixed probably with chopped straw, cow hair and dung. When the church or church loft needed repair the churchwardens paid not only for brick mortar and lime but hair as well.

In time the wattle and daub decayed and as bricks became cheaper they were used instead. This kind of infilling is called nogging. The bricklayers sometimes laid the bricks in the usual horizontal courses, sometimes in *chevron* or *herring-bone* pattern—or even vertically. During the eighteenth century bricks were used more and more. Timber-framed houses often had chimneys of brick because the risk of fire was very great and bricks resisted heat. By the end of the century walls were usually made of brick, and roofs of tiles. Sir Francis Dashwood, as you have read in Chapter 1, had the church of St Lawrence rebuilt in flint, but this was not normal practice. He also arranged for flint to be used in a Palladian house north of the High Street, and for a sham ruin resembling a church, which forms the entrance to caves dug into the side of the hill. Some houses in the parish have walls of brick and flint. The brick was used at the angles of the buildings, for window surrounds and chimneys, and the flint for forming panels within the brickwork. The flints come from the chalk of the Chilterns and from soil known as clay-with-flints.

The church loft on the north side of the street, the most interesting building in the village, is timber-framed. It was first built between 1400 and 1500, and has an overhanging upper storey. In Chapter 4 you read how the upper room was used for the Vestry meetings. The people in the village also attended services there when the weather was too bad for a climb to the church of St Lawrence on top of the hill.

The church loft as it looks today. Notice the timber frame and the bricks in between

The four rooms on the ground floor were divided by partitions of wattle and daub, (also mentioned on p. 69). In the eighteenth and nineteenth centuries, these were let to the poor, usually widows.

The infilling between the timbers is of bricks of various dates, many of them old. The size of bricks, particularly their thickness, helps us to tell their age. From 1500 to 1600 the average size of a brick seems to have been 9 inches by $4\frac{1}{2}$ inches by $2\frac{1}{4}$ inches. By 1700 the average thickness had grown to $2\frac{1}{2}$ inches and when in 1784 a tax was put on bricks by the thousand, brickmakers increased the thickness, generally to $3\frac{3}{4}$

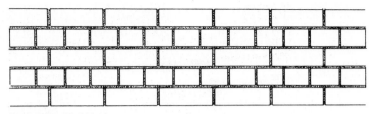

English Bond bricklaying

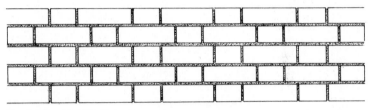

Flemish Bond bricklaying

inches. Another sign of the age of brickwork is the way in which the bricks were laid. Bricks laid with their sides to the wall-face are called 'stretchers' and those with their ends to the wall-face, 'headers'. In early brick walls there was often no regular plan: bricklayers laid bricks with their ends or their sides to the wall-face according to whim producing an irregular pattern. Between 1600 and 1700 the fashion grew of laying a course of headers followed by a course of stretchers, followed by another course of headers. This way of laying bricks was called 'English Bond'. During the eighteenth century bricklayers changed from English Bond to Flemish Bond in which each row of bricks had both 'headers' and 'stretchers', each header having a stretcher on each side of it and above and below.

In Church Lane, which is reached through an arch beneath the upper storey of the church loft, stands the old vicarage. It was originally built before the eighteenth century and although today the front of the house is of brick with only one piece of timber visible, many of the walls dividing one room from another have timber framing and some of the infilling 71

This is a photograph of the house in Church Lane described on the opposite page.
Notice the fire mark above the porch

is of wattle and daub. It seems that between 1724 and 1763
the vicarage was given a 'face-lift'—a new front in brick which
hid most of the original timber-framing. There are other houses
too in West Wycombe which have an eighteenth-century brick
front, with the original timber-framing clearly seen at the back.

Some houses, newly built during the eighteenth century, have the date on them. In Church Lane is a small house with the date 1722 on the front and the figure of an angel's head over the doorway. The small house dated 1722, shows several features in fashion when it was built. It has a symmetrical front: that is to say, the door is in the middle and the number of windows on each side of it is the same. Some of the window frames are straight and some curved. The windows themselves are sash windows sliding up and down by means of *pulleys*, not casement windows hinged on one side opening inwards or outwards. Above the doorway is a bricked up window. The reason for bricking up a window was usually, but not always, to avoid paying tax, because from 1696 to 1851 tax had to be paid according to the number of windows in a house. The house has steps leading to a raised ground floor. Below this floor was a basement, in which kitchen, dairy and larder might have been and any servants might have lived. A basement could well have been the workshop for a craftsman. The next two houses each bear the date of 1735 and initials or a name cut into a brick near the door. Three of the houses on this side of Church Lane have fire marks, small metal plates with the name of the insurance company responsible for the building or its contents—Sun, Royal Exchange, County. As few houses in the eighteenth century had a formal address a fire mark made it clear that the house was insured and with which company.

Some fire marks fixed before 1800 had numbers and where there is a number on a Sun Company mark which can be read, this gives us a good clue to follow, for the Sun Company still keep the old policies and can tell us a lot about the people who lived in these houses.

On the front of No. 17 High Street is the Sun Office fire mark 98143, the number of the policy which tells us that in 1745 Thomas Clarke, baker and grocer, insured his household goods, *utensils* and *stock-in-trade* in his new dwelling house, shop and *brewhouse* in brick stone and tile, for £200. The fire mark on the Swan inn leads us to a policy of 1749 by which

Two eighteenth century metal candleholders. The one on the left would have been hung from the ceiling, the one on the right would hold a rushlight and a candle

A skillet

Joan Swain of the Swan in West Wycombe insured her new dwelling house, brick and tiled for £80, her brewhouse for £15, her household goods, utensils and stock-in-trade for £80, her stables for £20, one tenement, brick, timber and tiled for £45. A Sun Office fire mark on a house on the north side of the street refers to policy 67434 by which in 1736 William Spencer insured the Black Boy Inn which is on the south side. Fire marks to-day are not always on the building on which they were originally placed.

INSIDE THE HOUSES

Lists of the church property made in 1706 and 1724 tell us about the inside of the vicarage. On the ground floor 'were a parlour, floored with boards, one hall laid with pavements (paving stones), one entry or passage, paved with bricks, one *buttery*, paved with bricks, one little hole to hold drink, floored with earth'.

The parlour with a boarded floor was drier and warmer than the rooms paved with bricks, earth or pavements, and here the vicar and his family sat and took their meals. A century before, it contained a 'great table' and two 'joined forms' (benches) and these may have still been there in 1724. Drink would be kept in the little hole floored with earth and in the buttery the vicar would probably store food and certainly saucers, basins, a *colander*, salt-cellars, spoons, quart and pint pots, drinking cups, barrels, pewter vessels of various sizes and for various purposes, and perhaps pewter candlesticks. The five upper rooms, one very small, all floored with board, were bedrooms. The outhouses were one woodhouse floored with earth, a stable of flint, a 'necessary house' floored with boards: all three outhouses were covered with tiles. By 1763 there was also a brewhouse, with a vat in which beer had to brew for several days.

In 1730 William Buckland, although unable to write his own name, and Robert Tilbury, overseers of the poor of West Wycombe, made an inventory of all the goods of Daniel Oxlade who had died. Downstairs were a dwelling room and a buttery and upstairs a little chamber and a bedroom. In the dwelling room were two small tables, ten chairs, a warming pan, fire shovel, tongs, bellows, a small cooking spit, a candle box two candlesticks and a bacon rack. The buttery contained, among other things, '3 drink vesells' two large iron 'potage potts' for cooking soup, one kettle, 3 'skillatts' (small pans with handles and legs which stand in the embers of a fire) and a trencher (wooden plate). The overseers found 'in the Roome over the dwelling house one feather bead and bedstead curtons a rug and three blackards (blankets) and 2 pairs of sheets two chestes a pare of bellows and other things'.

Eighteenth-century wills do not give details of all the goods of the person making the will but they do mention prized possessions. The will of Mary Pontyfix, made in 1768, says: 'I give and bequeath unto my said son Joseph Pontyfix my silver Watch and case which was his late Fathers and also my large Mahogany *claw table*...'

Anne Hurls (whom you have read about already in Chapters 2 and 3) mentioned a mahogany table when in 1782, 'being sick and weak in Body, but of sound Mind', she made her will:

> I give and bequeath unto my Daughter Martha the Bed, Bedstead, Bedding and other Furniture there to belonging that stands in the Room next immediately over the Hall: also the Settee, Bedstead, Quilt, Blankets.... To whom I further give and bequeath the oaken chest with all the Linen therein, that now stands in the Room over the Kitchen, with my Silver Watch, a Pair of Silver Salt Cellars, my Silver Punch Ladle and Silver Cream pot. I also give unto my said Daughter Martha the *Pier Glass* that now hangs over the Bureau in the Hall, together with the Mahogany Claw Table and the Mahogany dining Table in the same Room.
>
> And I give unto my Daughter Anne, my Silver Half Pint and Silver *Snuff Box*. All my China, Rings, Wearing Apparel, and the Horse hair Chairs in the Hall, I give to be Divided equally between my said Daughters...unto my Son James my Silver Tankard.

6   Rich and Poor Meet Together

HOW LONG DID PEOPLE LIVE?

As long ago as 1538 Thomas Cromwell, representing King
Henry VIII, ordered the clergyman of each parish to enter
in a book every wedding, christening and burial. These registers help us to try to answer such questions as 'How long did
people of the eighteenth century live?' 'Did the rich live longer
than the poor?' Sometimes the clergyman entered in the
register of burials more than the name of the person who had
died: he might add age, occupation, names of the parents of
a child, or special circumstances of the death. Can you read
the pieces on page 78 which come from the West Wycombe
parish register of burials?

Anne Hurls, overseer of the poor in 1779, who lived at Flint
Hall Farm and whose will you have just read about was
seventy-six years of age when she died, as her gravestone in
the churchyard of the church of St Lawrence on the hill tells
us. William Winter Lawrance, receiver of rents for the lord
of the manor and parish clerk from 1752 until his death in
1780, seems to have lived for seventy-three years. In the year
of his death, while he was churchwarden as well as parish
clerk, his signature to the vestry minutes was no longer in a
firm clear hand, which tells us that he was getting old.

John Hill, William Wade, Elenor Randall, Anne Hurls,
William Winter Lawrance and Sir Francis Dashwood him-
self (seventy-three) lived to a good age. Other ages on tomb-
stones are Jane Dean sixty-four, Elizabeth Barrabee forty,
Richard Fince fifty, William Neighbour fifty-six and his wife
Martha sixty-nine, Richard Hurls fifty-nine, John Carr sixty-

William Wade y: Tanner of this Town
Was Buried y: 8th day of January Aged 93 years

Matthew Youstise a poor Travelor
that dyed Upon whelerend Comon.
Buried y: 9th day of January 1712/13

William Parkins son of Willm parkins
Was Buried y: 15 day of Febrnary

Ann Beckley Wid: Buried y: 17th of Feb:

Burialls for y: Year 1713

a child
Hezekiah a keen Buried y: 31 of march

The Wife of Isaac Carter als Ruuening
Buried y: 9: of April 1713

Mary y: Wife of William Chalfant Was Buried
the 9th day of may in y: Year 1713

Sara y: daur: of Daniell Hill Buried y: 29 of June

Andrew Chilton, Buried y: 4th of october

Henry Balding Buried y: 15 of october

Elenor y: Wife of Edward Randall
Buried y: 20th of oct, Aged 84 years

Alice East wid: of the parish
of Crowell Buried nouember y: 22

nine, and his wife Ann seventy-four. But many children died before reaching the age of five, some at birth. Children born in a village in the eighteenth century would, on average, live for about thirty years. Girls born in the 1970s will live, on the average, seventy-three years and boys sixty-eight.

Opposite is part of a page of the register of burials for 1768-69. On the whole of the page, forty-one burials are recorded, including that of the wife of the lord of the manor, Sarah Baroness le Despencer: twenty-three of them were of children. Four of the entries were similar to the one 'a Stillborn Child of Francis and Grace Marshall put into the ground' referring to babies already dead when they were born. The words 'put into the ground' shows that the child had died unbaptised.

Smallpox caused the death of many children and adults. Throughout Europe in the eighteenth century it may have killed as many as 60 million people. Eighty out of every 100 of the people of Europe caught the disease sometime in their lives and those who remained alive might be blinded, disfigured, their faces *pock-marked*, or maimed for the rest of their lives. The accounts of the overseers of the poor of West Wycombe for 1715 tell the sad story of Henry Lawrence and his wife, both victims of smallpox, and how the villagers cared for them.

In 1734 the accounts recorded a similar story of Elenor Smith. When she had been buried the churchwardens paid 'The Harris wife for Cleaning and Airing Elenor Smith house' and for keeping her daughter for 2 weeks and airing her house. Other illnesses we find are 'being taken with the dead palsy', 'being lame', 'being sick and troubled with fitts'. Villagers who had met with accidents received money for a broken arm or leg, for 'Having put her Elbow out of joynt, for being run over with a cart'.

When Dr Bell and Dr Slater agreed with the vestry, for £10. 10s a year 'to attend find and provide all the poor of the parish (being parishioners) with proper physic and Medicines', they made it clear that for this fee they would not treat broken bones and smallpox. Dr Bell, 'Surgeon, *Apothecary*, and an Alderman' of High Wycombe, believed in inoculation and inoculated over 4,000 people. Ordinary people had noticed that if a person brought smallpox on himself perhaps by touching another who was already ill with the disease, he was less likely to die than if he waited for smallpox to strike him. Inoculation usually caused a mild case of the disease. Doctors inoculated by making a slight cut in an arm and drawing an infected cotton thread through it. As the eighteenth century was ending, Dr Jenner began to *vaccinate* young and old against smallpox. Vaccination in West Wycombe came in the next century.

TREATMENT FOR THE SICK

There were very few real remedies for the sick even among the rich. Henry Lawrence and his wife received milk and sack, an imported white wine, sometimes mixed with hot milk, cream, *mead* or *whey* to make medicinal drinks for invalids. Hartshorn, made by scraping, slicing or burning the horn of a hart, was a stimulant to give energy even for a short time. Dissolved in water, it was used as smelling salts, known as sal volatile. Diascordium was one of many medicines made of herbs. Widow Beasley and good wife Pusey received money from the overseers of the poor for nursing Henry Lawrence and his wife and keeping his children. At other times the overseers bought for the sick milk, bread, meat, cheese and a small barrel of weak beer.

Sometimes the vestry allowed patients to go to a doctor or surgeon and paid the bill, as for example, John Pearce in 1747, although they refused a request from Joseph Burden. In 1751 the vestry gave an order for George Dorrell to go to Dr Clark, paid William Burnham's surgeon's bill and agreed to pay Edward Keen's surgeon a guinea 'at Easter next'. People who were not doctors were paid for treating patients: Thomas Low was paid for *bleeding* Daniel Beaden, Mrs Shrimpton 'for setting Phelp's child's arm, and Mary Grange 'for curing John Young's Legg'. Occasionally the vestry agreed to hospital treatment.

West Wycombe records tell us little about treatment for illness which the middling sort and the rich could obtain. Some at least could afford to pay for the nursing, milk, sack, small beer, hartshorn and other medicines which the overseers provided for the poor. Some would pay for inoculation against smallpox: the vicar in 1766 paid £1 1s for 'Sally for her

Two eighteenth-century advertisements for medicine

inoculation'. If West Wycombe was like other places the countryfolk would know of charms and spells, of horrible 'cures' like the swallowing of lice, pills of cobwebs and slit earthworms; they would know of more effective folk medicine, discovered by experience and handed down from one generation to another, like the use of *foxglove* for a bad heart condition; they would know, again from experience, that a person who had had cowpox was unlikely to catch smallpox; they also knew of the value of herbs and simple care for invalids. For the rich, the doctors—who had few drugs of any value which they could use—usually advised purging, sweating and the taking of blood from a vein as the best treatment for most illnesses. When the Vicar was bled in this way by a Mr Wainwright, he paid a fee of 5s. Because many of the rich of the eighteenth century ate and drank far too much the treatment may have done some good. But their wealth attracted *quack* doctors, who had very little medical knowledge or skill, and were willing, for a fee, to prescribe powders, drops and pills which were of little use, and might have been harmful. 81

Octr 22 Willm Purkings of Woodbourne Bucks & Elizabeth
    Wheeler of Chinnor Oxon.

Nov 19 John Doll of Hugendon & Mary Strafford of this Parish.

Dec 30 Richard Brookland of Wantage Berks & Anne Maide
    of this Parish

Jan 6 Mr Thos Tilliard of the Parish of St Georges Hanover Square
    and Elizabeth Russell of this Parish

1740

Sept 15 Thomas Dorsett of prince Resborough & Jane Hood of
    this Parish

    23 John Browne & Eliz: Page both of this Parish

    25 Willm Neighbour & Martha Dorrell both of this Parish

Octr 2 Daniel Hickman of the Parish of Overton Wilks Shier &
    Sarah Sanders of the Parish of Hawley Bucks

Nov 26 Willm Ecker & Eliz morris both of this Parish

1741

March 31 John Hawes & Eliz: Arnat both of this Parish

May 14 John Browne the Elder & Mary Tomkins both of this Parish

June 5 John Scott of the Parish of Oxenton in the County of
    Northampton & Jane Harris of this Parish

    23 Robert

July 2 Edward Ford & Hannah Sears both of this Parish

Octr 6 James Joshua of the Parish of Bray in the County of Berks &
    Anne Smith of the Parish of Bledlow in the County of Bucks

    18 Thomas Garrett of Chipping Wycombe & Mary Harmon of the
    Parish of Great Marlow in the County of Bucks

Dec 1 James Weils & Mary Goodyer both of this Parish

    14 The Revnd Mr Sleigh Burdett of Wotton Bucks & Mrs Mary Browne
    of this Parish

    25 Thomas Chitten of Aylesbury & Susannah Mead of the
    Parish of Hugendon both in Bucks

Above, you can see part of a page from the register of marriages of the parish of West Wycombe for 1739 to 1741. Of the nine couples married you will notice that both bride and bridegroom in three of the marriages were of the parish of West Wycombe, that in four of the marriages, only the bride was of the parish and that in the other two marriages both bride and bridegroom came from other parishes.

Usually bride or bridegroom, or both, lived in the parish and the priest read the *banns of marriage* in the church on three Sundays, one after the other, before the wedding. A couple wishing to marry in a parish in which neither of them lived should have obtained a licence from a bishop or archdeacon. But some priests were willing to marry any couples who asked them to, for the fee.

In 1753 Parliament passed Lord Hardwicke's Marriage Act which ordered all churchwardens to provide 'proper books of *vellum* or durable paper' for the keeping of records of banns as well as marriages. The bride, the bridegroom, the priest,

Banns of Marriage *between John Morris and Ann Stra both of this Parish was published Nov.' 7. 14. & 21. 1756.*

Nº 19.

John Morris ———— of *this* Parish *Labourer*
_____ and *Ann Stra* _____ of *this*
Parish _____ were
Married in this *Church* by *Banns* _____ thi
25 ———— Day of *November* ———— in the Year One Thousand Seven
Hundred and *fifty six* _____ by me *W. Wroughton* .
This Marriage was solemnized between Us { *John morris* }
In the Presence of *The Mark ✝ of Joseph Stevens* { *The mark of ✝ Ann Stra* }
Will.ⁿ Winter Lawrance

and two witnesses had to sign one of the printed forms, which, four to a page, formed a bound volume. The example shown above had the signatures of the vicar, W. Wroughton, the bridegroom, John Marris, who although he was a labourer, could write his name, and William Winter Lawrance, our friend the parish clerk. The bride and one of the witnesses 83 could not write their names and had to put a cross.

If we look at the first twenty marriage entries after the Act of Parliament came into force we see that only eleven out of forty could sign their names, seven bridegrooms and four brides.

Between 1753 and 1800 there were 468 weddings in the church of St Lawrence on the hill. In all these marriages bride and bridegroom, or one of them, lived in the parish of West Wycombe, with one exception.

LEARNING TO READ, WRITE AND ADD UP

How did those who could sign their names learn to write? Their parents, employers, friends, a schoolmaster, a schooldame or writing master may have taught them. For some time the first Sir Francis Dashwood, lord of the manor, paid £12 a year to have twelve boys taught but the payment ceased before he died in 1724. Some of the boys and girls of West Wycombe were able to read at least, through the kindness of Katherine Pye. She had received from her sister, Quash Farm and the right to graze six cows, one bull, three horses and forty-five sheep in the common fields of Towersey, a parish a few miles from West Wycombe. In 1713 she entrusted the farm and common rights to twelve trustees who included Sir Francis Dashwood and the vicar of West Wycombe. From the rents and profits they were 'for ever' to pay 'Some schoolmaster, schooldame or schooldames to teach twenty poor boys and girls, or either or both, that should be children of the poor inhabitants' of the parishes of West Wycombe and four other nearby parishes. The schoolmaster or schooldame was to receive 3s for every boy or girl that should be taught to know all the letters of the alphabet, 'when so taught but not before'. He or she was to receive similarly 6s for each child who could 'spell English', 11s for each child who could 'read English' and say perfectly by heart the *catechism* of the Church of England. The second part of the *charity* was for boys only. The trustees had to appoint 'some good writing master or masters' to teach ten boys from the five parishes to write

84

Two schoolrooms in the eighteenth century

well, and cast accounts so well as to be made perfectly to understand the five fundamental rules of arithmetic, that is to say, numeration, addition, subtraction, multiplication and division. For each boy taught, the writing master received £1. 12s by stages and from his pay he had to provide each boy with pens, ink and paper.

Some West Wycombe parents may have sent their boys to the grammar school in the town of High Wycombe, 2½ miles 85 away, a school begun in the reign of Queen Elizabeth I. Grammar schools made a special point of teaching Latin and perhaps a little Greek. A boy who wished to become a scholar or a clergyman would find a grammar school education very helpful. In Great Marlow, a parish to the south of West Wycombe, Borlase school gave opportunities for training of another kind. A schoolmaster received £12 a year to teach twenty-four boys to write, read and cast accounts. The boys entered the school at ten to fourteen years of age and after they had been in the school for two years six boys were chosen to receive £2 to be apprenticed to a trade. Twenty-four girls, 'poor women children', learned to knit, spin and make bone lace.

CALAMITY AND VIOLENT DEATH

Many people, including a lord, a marquis, a bishop, other

The Humble Petition of MARY PONTIFEX *and* JOHN LEE, *of* Downley, *in the Parish of* West-Wycombe, *in the County of* BUCKS.

SHEWETH,

THAT on Saturday the Sixth of *November* last, a Fire broke out in the Stable of the said Sufferers, which entirely burnt down the said Stable, the Barn, and all other Outhouses, and consumed all the Stock of Corn, amounting to One Hundred and Thirty One Quarters of Barley, Four Horses, and Two Calves; which upon a just Estimate amounts to *Five Hundred and Two Pounds, One Shilling, and Sixpence.*

We beg leave farther to represent, that one of the Sufferers has been remarkably unfortunate; her Husband having been murdered some Years since in his return from Wycombe Market; and she herself left a Widow in very bad Circumstances with seven small Children.

It is therefore humbly hoped that the Publick will take these heavy Misfortunes into their Consideration, and afford such Relief as may in some Measure repair their losses, and enable them to continue their Business for the Support of themselves and Families.

gentry and clergy, and 'unknown hands' gave money to help Mary Pontifix and John Lee. The fire had broken out on

6 November 1756 and by June of the next year the amount given had reached £497, of which Sir Francis Dashwood had collected over £183 and the vicar of West Wycombe £9.

The churchwardens' accounts for the early part of the century record many gifts to people who had met with misfortune. As they went from village to village asking for help, they often carried letters of request.

Gentry, the middling sort and the labouring poor all dreaded fire as they dreaded smallpox. In 1756 fire destroyed several houses in West Wycombe village and nine years later two rooms in the mansion house of the lord of the manor. Sir Francis Dashwood, hoping to find a way to prevent fire from spreading in his house, covered part of the roof with copper plates and fixed thin iron plates between the ceiling of a ground floor room and the floor of a first floor room.

The petition of Mary Pontifix mentions the murder of her husband. Twenty years before the disastrous fire, two footpads, Marsh and Marshall, had waylaid him and his son as they walked home across fields on a January evening, from the Antelope Inn in High Wycombe to their farm at Downley. On Thomas Phillibrown's visit to the Wycombes in 1758 he was shown the field where the murder took place and heard how it happened. Marsh and Marshall who had been 'out eight days upon the *Pad*', followed father and son until they reached a stile, and having asked the way to West Wycombe, turned as if to go. Mr Pontifix, hearing the men again and looking round, saw Marsh about three yards away. Marsh, with long pistol or shot gun, fired without saying a word and the farmer fell dead. His son crawled through the bushes to fetch his mother and neighbours who found the body, watch and money gone. An offer of a reward for information was followed by the arrest of the two footpads at Rag Fair in London. In March, having been tried and condemned at the county town of Aylesbury, they made the sixteen mile journey to High Wycombe in a cart. When they arrived near the grammar school, a *gibbet* awaited them. As in other parts of the country, a public hanging attracted great crowds and it 87

A man hanged on a gibbet, with the crowds gathered to watch

would be interesting to know how many villagers from West Wycombe were in the crowd, which was so great that the pressure pushed down part of the school wall.

After this execution, the two rotting bodies, in chains, hung swaying in the wind, until complaints from members of the family of Lord Shelburne, whose house stood about half-a-mile away caused them to be removed.

In 1760 a highwayman who had murdered a Wycombe tradesman was to be hanged in the same way at the same place. Booths and stalls were set up on a nearby open space, to cater for the crowds expected. When the crowds heard that the hanging was not to take place in Wycombe after all, they got angry. But the hanging of 1736 was the last that the villagers of West Wycombe were to see at least within easy distance of their village.

How Do We Know?

In the possession of the present Sir Francis Dashwood, whose family have been lords of the manor for about 300 years, are estate maps, and a huge rent book from the eighteenth century. Many personal letters and papers of that time are in the Bodleian Library, Oxford and many deeds are in Buckinghamshire Record Office.

In Buckinghamshire Record Office, Aylesbury we can look at parish registers in which, from the time of Henry VIII, parish clergy kept records of all marriages, baptisms and burials which took place in their parish. The clergy and churchwardens also kept records of the parish vestry, accounts of the overseers of the poor, certificates of apprenticeship, removal certificates, certificates of settlement, wills and inventories, and we can also look at these.

The Buckinghamshire Record Office also has 'An Account of all the People in West Wycombe..... in 1760' and 'A Register of the Names and Occupations of all Persons......between the Ages of Fifteen and Sixty Years.....1798'. You may find similar documents in your own local Record Office or Public Library.

Things To Do

1. Find out more about Robert Adam and Capability Brown.
2. What kind of clothes did people, rich and poor, wear in the eighteenth-century?
3. The winter of 1708 was a very cold winter: a severe frost began on 7 January and lasted for three months. How do you think a family living in a cottage on the edge of one of the commons of West Wycombe managed to keep alive?
4. What does the book tell you about Anne Hurls?
5. James Edsell, barber and periwig maker, lived in the village of West Wycombe. Describe the traffic and the travellers he would see in the village and the people visiting his shop.
6. If there is a Victoria County History of your county, you may find information about your manor or parish. (Although you live in a town, the district where you live may have been a village in the eighteenth century. If in that century it had a church, it was probably a village, the centre of a parish: if not, it was probably a hamlet in an outlying part of a parish).
   a) Who were the lords of the manor? Find what you can about them. Where was their mansion house?
   b) Was there an important road running through your parish? If so, was it made a turnpike road?
   c) Were any alterations made to the parish church in the eighteenth century? Are there any gravestones of people who lived in the eighteenth century?
   d) Was there a parish workhouse in the eighteenth century?
   e) What were the occupations of the people of your parish then?
7. Draw or paint an eighteenth-century wain or a mail-coach (the door and lower panels were always maroon, the upper panels black and the wheels Post Office red).

NOTE The answers to some of these questions may only be found in the original parish records. The vicar or rector of the parish may still have these or they may have been placed in the care of the county record office or library.

Glossary

alcove, arched recess

apothecary, a doctor or one who sold medicines

apparitor, messenger of the archdeacon's court

apprenticed, bound to an employer to learn a craft, art, trade or profession

archdeacon, church official next below a bishop

Bacchus, Greek god of wine

bacon rack, frame hanging from kitchen ceiling above fire on which bacon was laid and left for two or three months to dry

banns of marriage, announcement in church that two people are planning a marriage

bib and strings, cloth under chin to keep front clean, kept in place with tapes or ribbons

black magic, calling up devils

bleeding, taking blood from a person by opening a vein or using leeches

brewhouse, room with vat and other vessels for brewing beer

buttery, room for storing food and drink

carriage, wheeled vehicle for goods or people

cascade, waterfall

catechism, question and answer used for teaching

causeway, raised road across low place or water

chaise, a light open carriage for one or two persons, sometimes with a hood

charity, money given or left by will to help the poor

chevron, pattern of V upside down and repeated

church rate, money collected in a parish for repairing the church and for other necessary charges of the churchwardens

claw table, table with pillar rising from three claw-shaped feet

colander, a bowl with holes in it, used as a strainer in cookery

communion, church ceremony of the Lord's Supper or Holy Communion

communion rails, rails in front of altar in church at which those receiving communion (bread and wine) kneel *curate*, assistant to vicar

Daphne, nymph who was turned into a laurel bush

daub, clay or mud

dedication, solemn ceremony giving something to a particular person or people (here to pagan gods)

dormer, window placed upright on a sloping roof

dowel, pins of wood to keep two pieces of wood together

drover, cattle dealer, driver of cattle or sheep

felon, someone guilty of a crime

flash or *flush lock*, boards in weir or dam which could be moved to allow barges to pass through on the flow or flush of water

flint, hard kind of stone, steel-grey and white

folly, useless sham building

font, hollowed stone or vessel in church to hold water for baptism

footpad, man on foot lying in wait to rob passers-by

forecastle, short raised deck at front of ship

foulweather coat, a greatcoat which men wore from the middle of the century in place of a cloak which was popular before

foxglove, tall purple or white flowered plant

game, wild animals and birds hunted for sport; gamekeepers were employed to look after game and stop poaching

gentry, people classed next below the nobility

gibbet, gallows or upright post with arm from which bodies of executed criminals were hung in chains

glean, gather ears of corn left by reapers

groom, servant who looks after horses

grotto, imitation cave

hamlet, small village, especially one without a church

header, brick with end appearing on face of wall

herring-bone, bricks or tiles set on the slant in alternate rows to form a zig-zag pattern

higgler, dealer travelling from place to place

homicide, murder

horsehair, material woven from hairs from manes and tails of horses, used for covering chairs and other seats

house of correction, building in which people who had committed small offences were kept under strict discipline and given hard labour

hundred, several parishes grouped to make subdivision of county

husbandman, a man who farms, higher than a labourer but lower than a yeoman

joists, pieces of wood parallel, stretched from wall to wall to take floor boards or ceiling laths *keel pieces,* pieces of timber at bottom of ship running its whole length, on which framework of ship is built

lacebuyer, dealer who gave out thread and patterns and collected finished lace

lathe, machine for turning wood or metal

livery, special clothes worn by servants

mail-coach, coach with armed guard, organised by Post Office to carry mail from 1784

malthouse, building in which malt, an ingredient of ale made from grain, was prepared and stored

manor, house and important land of local landowner, the 'lord of the manor' having control over tenants through manor courts.

mead, alcoholic drink made from honey and water

meet, suitable

menagerie, wild animals in cages

militia, army of citizens rather than professional soldiers

mortise and tenon joint, a tenon is a projection at the end of a piece of wood shaped to fit into a mortise, a hole cut into another piece of wood

necessary house, usually an outbuilding or separate building; a lavatory

nogging, brickwork filling spaces between timbers of a timber-framed house

obelisk, tall square pillar tapering to pyramid

orang-outang, large long-armed ape from Borneo or Sumatra

pad, upon the pad, lying in wait to rob passers-by

palsy, shaking of the limbs caused by a disease of the nervous system

parish, area in the charge of a vicar or rector, with its own church; people living in a parish are parishioners

parish clerk, parish official appointed by vicar to help with church and its services

pauper, a poor person, a person helped from the poor rate

peck, dry measure equal to two gallons (9 litres)

petty constable, constable having charge of law and order in parish

phaeton, four-wheeled light open carriage

pier glass, upright looking-glass

ploughland, area of land from 80 to 200 acres (32 to 80 hectares)

poacher, person who takes game unlawfully

pock-marked, having face pitted and scarred after smallpox

poor rate, a local tax raised in the parish to help the poor

postcart, mail-cart, two wheeled vehicle drawn by one or two horses used for carrying mail

postchaise, closed travelling carriage hired from one posthouse to the next, the driver sitting on one of the horses *posthouse,* house usually an inn at which horses and carriages could be hired

postilion, driver who sat on one of the horses drawing a postchaise or private carriage

premier baronet of Great Britain, first baronet to be created after Act of Union, 1707

presented, taken to court

privateer, armed vessel having private persons as owner and officers

probity, honesty

pulleys, cord and grooved wheel

punch, drink made of wine or spirits, hot water or milk, sugar, spice or cordial

quack, one who pretends to be a doctor offering wonderful cures

rafter, roof timber sloping up from wall to ridge

relief, money given to the poor

rushlight, meadow rush dried and dipped in mutton fat, to give light when burning in metal holder

shift, undergarment, vest

snow, here means a small sailing vessel

snuff box, box for powdered tobacco for sniffing into nostrils

spit, metal bar or bars on which meat is made to revolve before a fire

squire, country gentleman, chief landowner

stag, male deer

stage-coach, coach giving regular service between towns with fixed stages (where passengers set down or picked up and horses changed)

statute labour, work on parish roads made compulsory by Act of Parliament (statute)

steward, one who acts for lord of the manor

stock-in-trade, all things necessary for a trade

stocks, wooden framework in public place with holes for offender's feet, or feet and hands, a punishment

stretcher, brick with side appearing on face of wall, in another sense part of chair or stool

stud, upright timber in timber-framed house

tenement, piece of land, dwelling-house

tie-beam, beam connecting the two slopes of a roof across its foot to prevent roof from spreading

toll, sum paid for use of a road or bridge

treadle, lever moved by foot giving motion to lathe or other machine

tripod, support with three legs

Turk's head, long handled broom with head of feathers for dusting

turnpike, gate where tolls were collected

urn, vase or receptacle with a supporting foot or pedestal

94   *utensils,* used in kitchen for cooking and serving food

vaccinate, put fluid from cowpox blister into scratch made in skin to prevent smallpox

vagrant, wanderer

valet, personal manservant

vellum, calf skin beaten very thin for writing on; also used, less thin for binding books

Venus, goddess of love

victualler, keeper of public house or inn

wadding, soft material placed in gun-barrel to keep gunpowder in place

wain, farm wagon

wallposts, main upright posts of timber-framed house reaching from foundations to roof

wattle, rods or twigs woven together

whey, watery liquid left when butter has been churned out of milk

yeoman, middle-class farmer

Acknowledgements

The author thanks Sir Francis Dashwood, Bart, to whom he is much indebted for access to documents and maps at West Wycombe, in the Bodleian Library and in Buckinghamshire Record Office, and for permission to take photographs in West Wycombe House and Park. The author also wishes to thank P.K. Ames for permission to quote extracts from the Phillibrown diary.